LOUISBOURG

✣ An 18th-Century Town ✣

A.J.B. Johnston
Kenneth Donovan
B.A. Balcom
Alex Storm

Cathy Lawrence
Paul Black
Annette Currie
Margaret Dicks
Ken MacDonald

Nancy Nicol
Sharon MacLeod
Charles MacMaster
André MacMullin
Gary MacNeil

Enterprise Cape Breton Corporation

NIMBUS PUBLISHING LTD

Nimbus Publishing
P.O. Box 9166, Halifax, Nova Scotia
B3K 5M8
(902) 455-4286

Cover design: Arthur Carter, Halifax
Cover photograph: Warren Gordon, Sydney

Text by Louisbourg historians A.J.B. Johnston, Kenneth Donovan, B.A.
Balcom, Alex Storm, and the following teachers of the Cape Breton District
School Board: Paul Black, Annette Currie, Margaret Dicks, Cathy Law-
rence, Ken MacDonald, Sharon MacLeod, Nancy Nicol (elementary
curriculum supervisor), Charles MacMaster, André MacMullin, Gary
MacNeil

Financial Support: Enterprise Cape Breton Corporation, Sydney. ECBC is a
development agency committed to economic growth and industrial
diversity on Cape Breton.

Canadian Cataloguing in Publication Data

Johnston, A.J.B.

Louisbourg

For use in Grades 5-7.
ISBN 0-921054-88-2
1. Louisbourg (N.S.)—History—Juvenile literature. I. Title.
FC2314.L68J63 1991   971.6'95501   C91-097562-0 F1039.5.L8J63 1991

Enterprise   *Société*
Cape Breton *d'expansion*
Corporation *du Cap-Breton*

Fortress/Forteresse
of   de
Louisbourg

CAPE BRETON DISTRICT SCHOOL BOARD

TABLE OF CONTENTS

FOREWORD

Louisbourg: An 18th-Century Town offers an in-depth look at what was once a well-known settlement in the New World. As a seaport, Louisbourg possessed one of the busiest harbours in North America. As a fortress, it generated hope in French hearts and fear in British ones. As a community, it was home to thousands of men, women, and children: fishermen and soldiers, merchants and artisans, servants and seamstresses. Voltaire called the colony "the key" to French possessions in North America. Benjamin Franklin described it as a "tough nut to crack." In the end, British prime minister William Pitt insisted that it be destroyed. Pitt got his wish, yet 200 years later, 18th-century Louisbourg rose again, this time as one of the world's great outdoor museums.

Although its life was short, Louisbourg had a rich and complex history. In this book, that history is organized into three thematic sections: The Fortress, The Seaport, and The Community. Each of these sections, in turn, contains short chapters on selected topics. Prepared in co-operation with teachers from the Cape Breton District School Board, *Louisbourg: An 18th-Century Town* offers the reader an educational text that entertains. In its well-illustrated pages is material on everything from astronomy to gardening, from fashions to siege warfare. Along the way, there are puzzles and quizzes, assorted activities, and even a few recipes. So settle back and discover the world of 18th-century Louisbourg.

INTRODUCTION

The story of 18th-century Louisbourg cannot be told without mentioning war. The town was founded at the end of one war, suffered defeat in a second, and then largely faded from history at the conclusion of a third.

The French came to Louisbourg in 1713, at the end of the War of the Spanish Succession. Under the terms of the treaty that ended that conflict, France ceded to Great Britain its territory in what are now Newfoundland and mainland Nova Scotia. France retained Île Royale (Cape Breton Island) and Île St.-Jean (Prince Edward Island).

The settlement that became Louisbourg started out as a simple base for the cod fishery. But as the town prospered and trade grew (with France, the West Indies, Québec, New England, and Acadian settlements in Nova Scotia), Louisbourg developed into one of the most important ports in New France. By the 1730s, more than 150 ships were sailing into Louisbourg harbour every year, making it one of the busiest seaports in North America. By the 1740s,

Louisbourg's year-round population ranged from 2 500 to 3 000. Hundreds more arrived during each shipping season.

Because of its economic and commercial importance, Louisbourg emerged as the administrative centre for Île Royale and Île St.-Jean. At the same time, Louisbourg became the main French military stronghold in the Atlantic region. As a fortress, it resembled a European fortified town: it was completely enclosed by walls and had batteries and outer works as well. In North American terms, this *ville fortifiée* (fortified town) ranked among the most heavily defended settlements on the continent.

Louisbourg's inhabitants were mostly French; that is, they were men, women, and children from France, Acadia, the settlements along the St. Lawrence River, or the French West Indies. Yet some of the people of Louisbourg also came from other cultures. The town was home to several hundred Basques, as many as 150 Germans and Swiss, and smaller numbers of Irish, English, African and, occasionally, Micmac peoples.

In 1745, after three decades of peace and prosperity, Louisbourg was attacked and conquered by a combined British and New England force. Its citizens were deported to France, and the town was occupied by an enemy army. Four years later, after the terms of the Treaty of Aix-la-Chapelle (1748) gave Île Royale back to France, the French returned to Louisbourg.

For nearly a decade, the inhabitants of Louisbourg once again led peaceful and prosperous lives. Then, during the Seven Years' War (1756-63), the British came again. They captured Louisbourg for a second and final time in 1758. Once more, the French soldiers and settlers were sent back to France. With Louisbourg eliminated as a strategic stronghold and naval base, the British went on to conquer Québec (1759) and Montréal (1760). The Treaty of Paris in 1763 confirmed that New France had become part of British America.

The fall of New France spelled the end of Louisbourg as a fortress, community, and seaport. The once formidable bastion of New France faded quickly from the world scene. The British systematically demolished its fortifications in 1760 and withdrew the last of their garrisons in 1768. For the next century, Louisbourg was little more than an isolated fishing village, remarkable only for its "heaps of stones"—the ruins of what had once been historic 18th-century Louisbourg.

THE FORTRESS
Louis

THE FORTIFICATIONS

When people think of Louisbourg, they often think of
high walls looming in the fog, or sentries guarding
one of the town gates, or a solitary soldier standing on
the ramparts. What people today may consider
picturesque, however, the people of the 18th century
regarded as essential. "But of course," the long-ago
residents would have said, "every stronghold has to
have its walls and soldiers and its gates and ramparts.
Those things are there to defend us."

This section discusses Louisbourg's fortifications:
what they were, how they were built, and their
strengths and weaknesses.

bourg

LOUISBOURG AS A FORTIFIED TOWN

One's initial impression of Louisbourg's fortifications depends largely on one's experiences. This was also true in the 18th century.

The New England soldiers who besieged the fortress in 1745 thought Louisbourg was formidable. But then, few New Englanders had ever seen a fortification more elaborate than a blockhouse, a stockade fort, or perhaps an earthwork battery.

French visitors to Louisbourg, however, saw the town through different eyes. Used to the elaborate fortresses of Europe, in particular the strongholds of France, they thought Louisbourg was a simply fortified town.

The fortified town of Louisbourg. Plan, 1741.

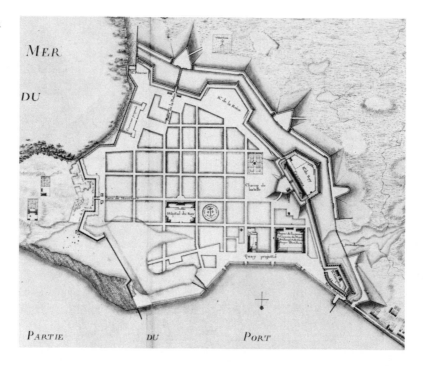

Still, on the North American continent, Louisbourg was one of the largest and most impressive military strongholds. Its defences took more than two decades to construct, and when at last they were finished, Louisbourg was a fully enclosed *ville fortifiée* (fortified town). No one could enter, except through one of its guarded gates. There were high walls on the landward side, and more than 100 cannons standing ready on the ramparts.

Louisbourg's high walls featured cannons on the ramparts.

THE FORTRESS CONTEXT

Louisbourg's defences were conceived and built according to the general fortification principles of the 17th and 18th centuries. These principles had been perfected in Europe by Sébastien Le Prestre de Vauban (1633-1707), the chief engineer of Louis XIV. Vauban constructed or modified more than 100 fortresses along France's borders.

The fortifications of the preceding era—the late Middle Ages—had called for castles, towers, and

Portrait of Vauban, painted by Rigaud.

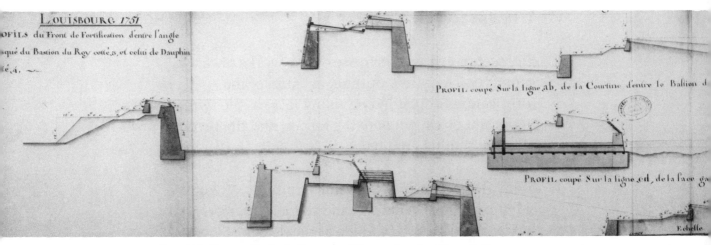

other high-walled defences. These had offered the most effective protection against catapults and scaling ladders.

French engineer's profile drawings of some of the fortifications.

With the introduction of artillery in the 16th century, however, those defences became outmoded. The high walls were vulnerable to cannons firing iron balls. A castle that had withstood countless attacks during medieval times could be reduced to rubble in hours by artillery fire.

The new approach to defence called for lower and thicker walls. These walls had to be protected or hidden from direct cannon fire. To achieve that protection, fortification engineers developed an earthwork called a "glacis." This glacis was gently sloped away from the fortress so that defenders could see approaching enemy soldiers.

The walls of the new defences were angled as well, to maximize the field of fire against attackers. These angles were carefully calculated by engineers. The most common shape used in these new defences was that of the bastion.

THE BASTION SYSTEM

Eighteenth-century fortresses were works of careful geometry. The actual outline, or trace, of the fortifications depended on many factors, the two most important of which were the terrain and the theories of the designing engineers.

Many defences were star-shaped; others were odd-sided polygons. Whatever the shape, engineers took care to calculate every angle at the design stage, to take maximum advantage of the terrain.

Common to almost every fortress were bastions. These were projections in the surrounding walls. A full bastion had two faces and two flanks. There were also half- or demi-bastions.

Engineers usually placed bastions close to each other, so that cannon and musket fire from one would protect the other. In larger fortresses, engineers added outer works—redoubts, ravelins, and demi-lunes—to give additional protection to the main walls. Some of Louisbourg's engineers proposed adding elaborate outer works to the town's defences, but a shortage of funds resulted in only the simplest earthworks being built.

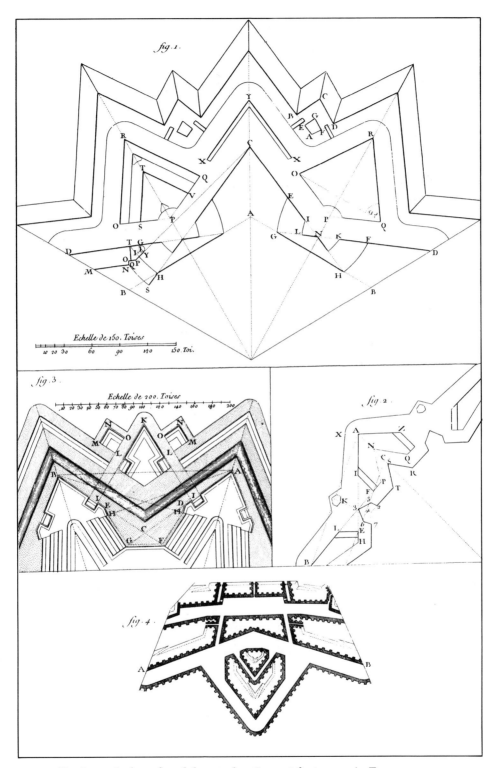

Engineers' plans for elaborate bastions at fortresses in France.

TERMINOLOGY

Fortification terminology is specialized, with dozens of terms. Listed are some of the more common ones.

Banquette   A step running inside the **parapet** that the troops stand on while firing.

Bastion   A projecting part of a fortification, usually having two faces that are connected to the **curtain** walls by two shorter walls called "flanks."

Demi-bastion   A **bastion** having one face and one flank.

Battery   A group of guns placed at regular intervals and used for combined action; also a platform for cannons.

Counterscarp   Wall limiting the ditch opposite the **escarp**.

Curtain   The part of the fortification wall that connects two **bastion**s.

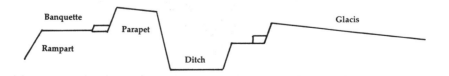

Embrasure   An opening in a **parapet** for a cannon. It is wider at the outer opening to allow maximum sweep while affording cover for the cannoneers.

Escarp   The exterior face of the **rampart**.

Glacis   A gently sloping earthwork, beginning at the outer works and stretching towards the countryside.

Palisade   Strong, pointed wooden stake. A number of them fixed deep in the ground and close together create a defensive work.

Parapet   A defence made of earth or stone to protect the troops and armament from the enemy's fire and observation.

Rampart   A massive bank of earth surrounding a defended position; the top of the rampart is known as the **parapet**.

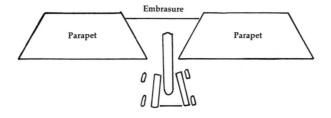

THE LOUISBOURG DEFENCES

When the French first settled on Île Royale, the name of Cape Breton Island between 1713 and 1758, colonial officials thought Louisbourg would be too difficult to fortify. The terrain was marshy, and there were no dominant hills on which to build a commanding fort.

It soon became apparent, however, that the fishery and trade were making Louisbourg the largest and most important settlement on the island. The town also became the administrative capital of Île Royale. Therefore, it had developed into a settlement that required major fortifications. It had to be transformed into a military stronghold.

Louisbourg's defences had two objectives. First, they had to protect the town. Walls were built, completely surrounding the settlement. The highest were located on the landward side and the lowest along the waterfront. In total, seven bastions and six curtain walls joined them.

Profile of Louisbourg's Dauphin Demi-Bastion area.

Second, Louisbourg's defences had to protect the harbour. For this purpose, various batteries were constructed. Two batteries were located inside the town—at either end of the waterfront—while two others protected the harbour entrance.

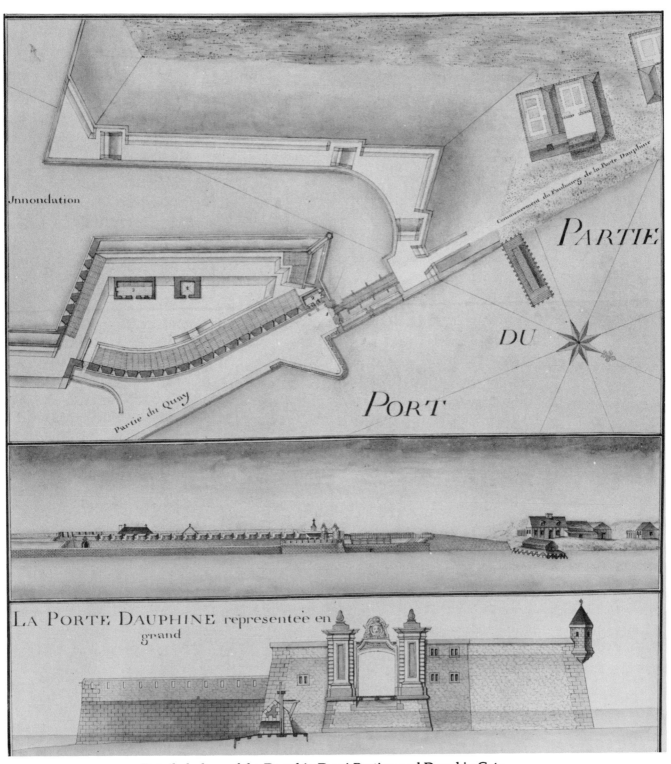

Detailed plans of the Dauphin Demi-Bastion and Dauphin Gate.

THE ENGINEERS

The responsibility for designing most French fortifications during the 18th century lay with the corps of engineers. Such was the case at Louisbourg as well.

Trained as architects, the King's Engineers (*ingénieurs du roi*) enjoyed the status of an elite group. At Louisbourg, they planned and supervised all the fortification work. They also designed the government buildings and devised the town plan.

While the engineers were important, they were few in number. Usually, there was one chief engineer who had several assistants.

Three particularly well-known engineers worked at Louisbourg. Beginning in 1717, Jean-François de Verville laid out the plan for the town and its defences. Verville then supervised the early years of construction.

Étienne Verrier succeeded Verville in 1725 and remained the chief engineer until 1745. Verrier oversaw the construction of landward and seaward fortifications, the lighthouse, and many King's buildings.

Louis Franquet, who served at Louisbourg during the 1750s, was responsible for the fortifications of all New France. This meant he spent part of his time at Louisbourg and part at Québec City. Franquet submitted many ideas on ways to improve Louisbourg's defences, but a lack of money in the Royal Treasury meant that few improvements were actually made.

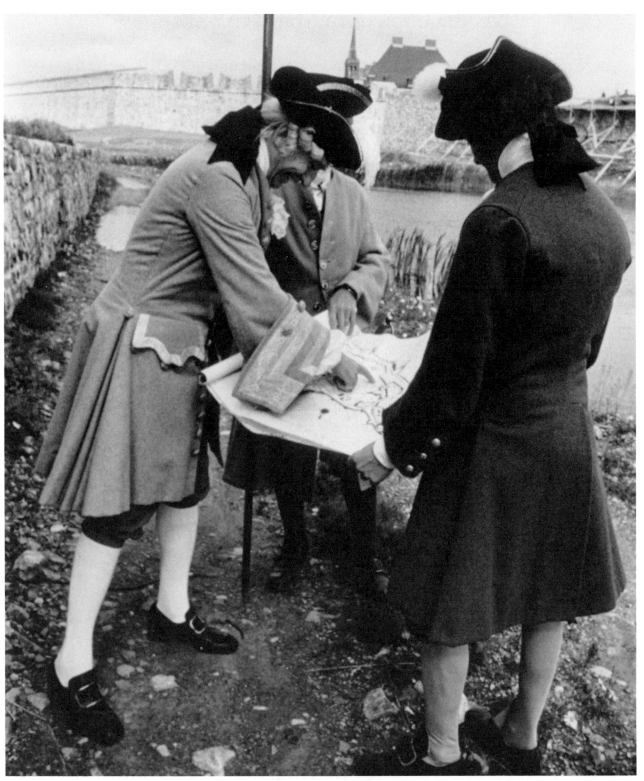

Louisbourg engineers examining a plan.

CONSTRUCTION OF THE FORTIFICATIONS

Civilian contractors from France built the fortifications and the King's buildings. Using the plans prepared by the King's Engineers, they hired the workers needed to do the job. Many of the tradespeople and labourers were soldiers in the garrison. The soldiers received extra pay for their work on the fortifications.

The builders faced two major problems. First, some of the lime mortar was of poor quality: it had a high sandstone content, which weakened it. Moreover, sea salt in the sand prevented the mortar from setting properly.

Second, Louisbourg, like many seaside towns, had a damp climate. The mortar took a long time to dry in the changeable, wet weather, and the frost-thaw cycle damaged the already-weak mortar.

Because of these problems, the French were forced to carry out continual repairs. They sometimes applied new mortar, but even more effective, they discovered, was nailing wooden planks to the stone walls. The French also used iron crampons, which looked like giant staples, to seal the stones into place.

Guérite, or sentry box, King's Bastion.

DEFENDING LOUISBOURG HARBOUR

As a major port of call, Louisbourg had to have a strongly defended harbour. The French feared a surprise attack by the British or the New England colonists. Several coastal defence works were erected around the harbour as protection against such an assault. The cannons of the fortress were mounted on naval carriages, the same as those found on board a ship. There were four batteries:

Royal Battery
Its field of fire was directed at the harbour and towards the entrance.

Island Battery
It also covered the harbour and the entrance, though from a different angle.

Pièce de la Grave Battery
Its cannons, too, swept parts of the harbour.

Semi-circular Battery
Its field of fire swept the harbour as well.

Island Battery (left), Royal Battery (right).

When speaking of a "field of fire," one must realize that accuracy declined dramatically the farther away the enemy target. The effective range of an 18th-century cannon was only about 1 500 metres, which is not far in modern terms. To hit and damage a moving target such as a ship, one had to be closer than that— or extremely lucky.

Plans showing the "fields of fire" on Louisbourg harbour.

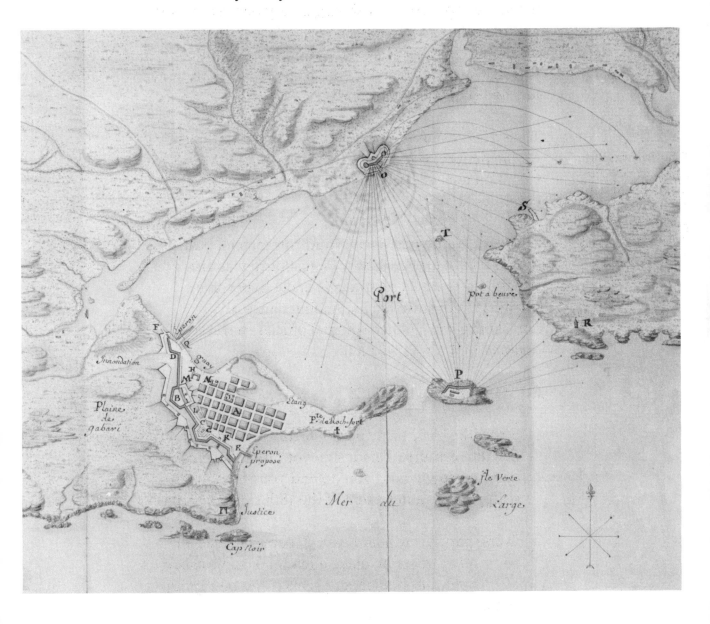

THE COST OF LOUISBOURG

Much has been said about the high cost of fortifying Louisbourg. Some writers believe that the money was foolishly spent. In the context of the era, however, that was not the case. The French wanted, and were willing to pay for, a strongly defended town. As well, the money spent on Louisbourg in any one year never exceeded the cost of outfitting a single warship for a six-month patrol of North Atlantic waters. Such patrols were considered essential, and so were well-fortified settlements on shore.

*The *livre* was the standard monetary unit of the Ancien Régime in France. The purchasing power of 1 *livre* roughly equalled 12 dollars (1989).

The actual cost of Louisbourg to the French treasury, for the period from 1713 to 1758, was 4 million *livres** (spent on fortifications) and 16 million *livres* (spent on other public works).

In return, France had a naval and commercial port, as well as a base for her fishery. Louisbourg was also a stronghold that served strategic ends. Expensive though the construction and maintenance of Louisbourg was, French colonial officials never doubted that it was worth it.

SUGGESTED ACTIVITIES

1. Study the basic principles of fortification design in the 18th century, then design your own defence system. How would you defend your hometown using the bastion system of the 18th century?

2. Using paper, cardboard, wood, papier maché, or some other material, make a model of some aspect of 18th-century Louisbourg. This could be a group project.

THE GARRISON

Like all fortified towns, Louisbourg required a large garrison. It needed soldiers to man its gates and guardhouses and to patrol its streets and walls. Even when off duty, the soldiers had to be close at hand in case of attack.

During the 1740s, soldiers made up about one-quarter of Louisbourg's population; that is, there were roughly 700 soldiers among the 2 500 to 3 000 inhabitants. During the 1750s, the military formed nearly one-half of the town's population. When the proportion of soldiers is that high, the community is called a "garrison town."

Wherever one went in Louisbourg, there were military activities. Sentries stood guard in front of various King's buildings, detachments of soldiers moved through the streets, sentinels patrolled the walls and stood at entry gates. There were military drum calls almost every hour.

The many garrison routines, along with the walls that enclosed the town, gave the people a feeling of order and security.

GARRISON ACTIVITIES

Throughout most of Louisbourg's history, the soldiers performed more construction work than military duties. The following, however, focuses on their military activities.

The military duties of the soldiers included:

Guard duty—This involved being assigned to a guardhouse or being posted as a sentry.

Town patrol—These soldiers were like police and helped keep order in the town.

Detachment or expedition duty—This included chasing deserters and fighting the enemy.

Ship duty—This involved standing guard on ships anchored in the harbour.

Basic drills—Soldiers practised firing muskets or cannons and marching.

The most common assignment was probably guard duty. There were five guardposts within the walls of the fortress and another two outside the walls (at the Royal and Island batteries). The soldiers assigned to these posts stayed there for 24-hour periods.

All soldiers on guard duty, including officers, had to remain near the guardhouse throughout their 24-hour shift. They also had to remain in uniform and have their weapons close at hand.

The sentries posted around the town came from the men assigned to the guardhouses. These sentries stood watch at key points in the fortress, as well as in front of certain King's buildings. In summer, sentries changed every two hours; in winter, every hour or at the discretion of the commanding officer. When not on sentry duty, the soldiers assigned to the guardhouse cut wood or cleaned their rooms.

Sentry standing guard in front of the King's Storehouse.

THE MILITARY UNITS

As one of France's many overseas colonies, Île Royale came under the jurisdiction of the Ministry of the Marine. The Marine department was also responsible for France's navy.

The troops that served in France's overseas colonies were the Ministry of the Marine's own forces. These were the *troupes de la Marine*, also known as the *compagnies franches de la Marine*, roughly meaning "independent companies of the Marine."

The Marine troops were recruited in France specifically for the colonies. According to regulations, the soldiers were at least 16 years old and about 1 metre 62 centimetres tall. In practice, however, both younger and shorter soldiers were sent to Louisbourg. Because Louisbourg required so much construction work, Marine officials tried to recruit soldiers who had special skills or trades.

Unlike the French army, Marine troops were not organized into regiments. Instead, they were grouped into independent companies. The number and size of the units varied widely. During the 1740s, there were eight companies with 70 men each. Each company was named after its captain: for example, Captain Michel DeGannes' unit was known as the DeGannes Company.

Not all Île Royale soldiers were stationed at Louisbourg. There were also small detachments at Port Dauphin (St. Anns) and Port Toulouse (St. Peters).

Sentry guarding the
Dauphin Gate.

Besides the Marine troops, the Louisbourg garrison had an elite group of artillery specialists known as the *canoniers-bombardiers*. They formed a separate company of 30 men. These specialists attended an artillery school while at Louisbourg and were in charge of the many cannons in the fortress.

Finally, there was a mercenary regiment of Swiss and German soldiers. This was the Karrer Regiment, named after its colonel, Franz Joseph Karrer. The Karrer detachment numbered up to 150 soldiers.

The Karrer troops felt they deserved special privileges. Some of these privileges were specified in their contract with the King; others were not and were the subject of dispute.

In December 1744, the French soldiers of Louisbourg mutinied against their officers. The soldiers complained of unfair treatment, and many mentioned poor food rations. The officers, however, blamed the Karrer soldiers for starting the protest. As a result, the Karrer Regiment was not sent back to Île Royale when it was reoccupied by the French in 1749, following the British capture of Louisbourg in 1745.

Flintlock musket

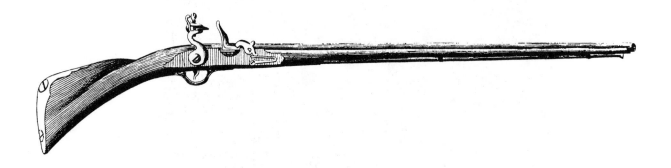

Left to right: A soldier from the *compagnies franches de la Marine*, a cannoneer, another Marine, and a soldier from the Karrer Regiment.

CROSSWORD PUZZLE

ACROSS

2. soldier who fights for money
4. branch of the army that uses cannons and mortars
5. soldier standing guard
6. permanent unit of an army, divided into companies, troops, or batteries
7. soldiers; armed forces

DOWN

1. troops stationed in a fortress or town
2. revolt by soldiers
3. newly enlisted soldier

SUGGESTED ACTIVITIES

1. Pretend you are an 18th-century soldier. Write a
    letter to your parents describing your life as a
    soldier at Louisbourg.

2. Draw a scene (or scenes) from a soldier's life at
    Louisbourg.

ANSWERS TO THE CROSSWORD PUZZLE

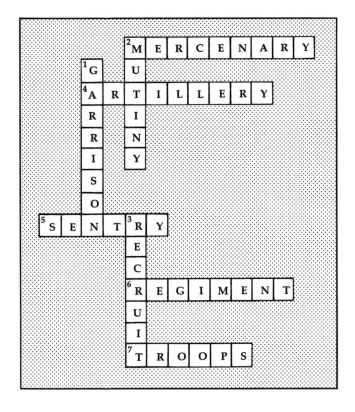

THE SIEGES

The best-known events in Louisbourg's history are its sieges, which are lengthy army assaults on a fortified position. Twice Louisbourg was besieged, and twice it fell.

BACKGROUND TO THE 1745 SIEGE—
THE SUMMER OF 1744

The first assault on Louisbourg occurred during a European conflict known as the War of the Austrian Succession (1740-48). This war had broken out when the Holy Roman Emperor died without leaving a male heir. Some European powers tried to seize Austrian lands, while others fought to keep the existing boundaries.

The war did not involve Louisbourg until 1744. In the spring of that year, the kings of France and Great Britain declared war on each other. This meant that the French and British colonies in North America were also at war. Soldiers, sailors, and townspeople of Louisbourg had to prepare for a possible attack by New England or British forces. Similarly, the British

Re-enactment of the posting of the 1744 ordinance declaring France
to be at war with Britain.

settlements on mainland Nova Scotia—Annapolis Royal and Canso—had to be on the lookout for a French attack.

Word of the outbreak of war reached Louisbourg in early May 1744. Governor Jean-Baptiste Le Prevost Duquesnel and his military officers swiftly planned an attack on the New England fishing base at Canso. On May 23, an expedition of 351 men, sailing in 17 vessels, left Louisbourg. The following morning, the tiny fleet arrived at Canso and began its assault. The settlers there were unaware that war had been declared, so they resisted only briefly and then surrendered.

Following the conquest of Canso, Louisbourg officials turned their attention to privateering. "Privateering" was a form of warfare at sea in which privately owned ships were licensed to attack and plunder enemy vessels.

Throughout late May and early June 1744, Louisbourg privateers captured many fishing boats and merchant ships from New England. As the summer progressed, however, British warships and New England privateers began to fight back, eventually gaining the upper hand. By September 1744, many French boats and ships had been taken as prizes.

In the war on land, the capture of Canso in May led the French to consider an assault on the only other British settlement in Nova Scotia: Annapolis Royal. The French launched two sieges against Annapolis Royal, one in July and one in the fall. But Louisbourg could not send the naval support necessary to force the British to surrender. Therefore, though twice attacked, Annapolis Royal did not fall to the French in 1744.

The events of 1744—the French capture of Canso, the privateering, and the two assaults on Annapolis Royal—led directly to the attack on Louisbourg in 1745. Having seen how vulnerable British settlements and ships were to attacks from Louisbourg, the New Englanders, under the leadership of Massachusetts governor William Shirley, decided to attempt the capture of the French fortress.

Cape Breton as Isle (Île) Royale, a colony of France. The arrow shows the route taken by the French fleet that attacked Canso in 1744.

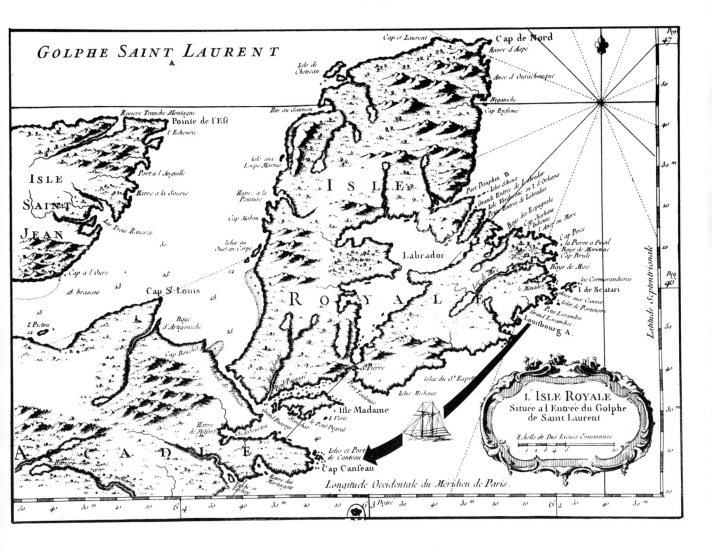

THE DECISION TO ATTACK—1745

In the spring of 1745, New England raised an army of more than 4 000 men for an expedition against Louisbourg. William Pepperrell of Kittery, Maine, was placed in command. Great Britain offered naval support, and New York, New Jersey, and Pennsylvania gave money, arms, and supplies.

The New England invasion fleet anchored down the coast from Louisbourg.

In April, the expedition set sail from the American colonies. It sailed first to Canso, to begin preparations for the assault on Louisbourg. At the same time, part of the British fleet set out to blockade the French port.

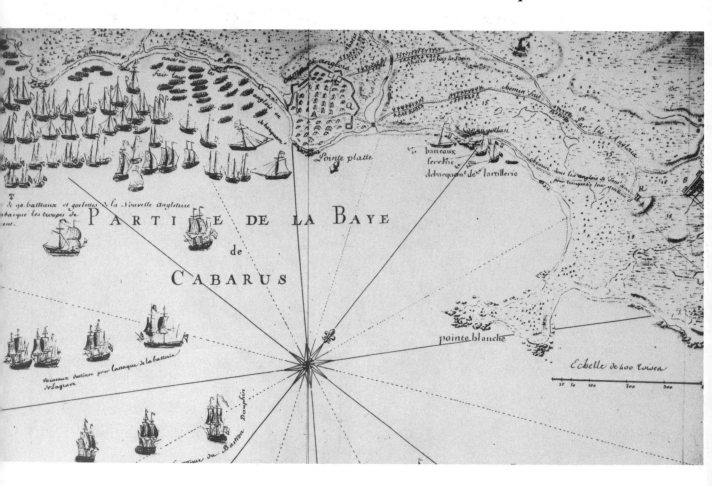

Spring drift ice delayed the attack for a while, but at last, by early May, conditions were right for the assault to begin.

THE DEFENDERS

During the first siege, Louisbourg's defenders had to deal with several weaknesses. First, troop morale was low because of the mutiny that had taken place the preceding winter. Second, the garrison itself numbered fewer than 700 soldiers, with perhaps another 900 militia—not a large force given the extent of the town's fortifications. Third, the defences had weak points: the Royal Battery was under repair, and there were hills close to the major bastions, from which enemy cannoneers could bombard the town. Fourth, Louisbourg was extremely vulnerable to a naval blockade. The port could survive only for as long as it had supplies. Without reinforcements or additional provisions, Louisbourg would fall.

THE ATTACKERS

The New England attack force approached the siege with strength and confidence. The land force consisted of approximately 4 000 soldiers organized into 11 regiments. For some of these soldiers, the assault on Louisbourg was a bit like a religious crusade. They saw themselves as militant Protestants setting out to capture a Roman Catholic stronghold.

The naval force numbered more than 100 vessels, the most impressive of which were 12 British warships. The British naval squadron was under the command of Sir Peter Warren.

SIEGE EVENTS

In the early morning of May 11, 1745, the British fleet entered Gabarus Bay. Within hours, the New Englanders landed. The French force sent from Louisbourg to oppose them was too small and too late. The next day, the French decided to abandon the Royal Battery. With the enemy safely ashore down the coast, there was little hope that the French could defend the battery against an attack from the rear. Before they left, however, they drove spikes down the touch holes of their cannons. They thought this would make them unuseable. On May 13, the New Englanders took over the battery and soon repaired the French cannons.

Besides taking over the Royal Battery, the besiegers established several new batteries of their own. As the siege progressed, the attacking cannon positions moved closer and closer to the fortress walls.

While the New Englanders captured the Royal Battery without a struggle, the same was not true of other French posts. A direct assault on June 6 against the Island Battery failed miserably, and the New Englanders suffered heavy loss of life. The attackers then changed their tactics and established a battery on Lighthouse Point, from which they could bombard the Island Battery. They succeeded, and the French cannons on the island fell silent on June 24. Two days later, all firing ceased, and the two sides negotiated the terms of surrender. On June 27, an agreement was reached. The New Englanders entered the town the following day with "Colours … flying, the Drums Beating, Trumpets Sounding, Flutes & Viols Playing."

According to the conditions of surrender, the French were permitted to keep many of their possessions. Within a few weeks, nearly all the inhabitants of Louisbourg boarded ships headed for France, where they would stay until a peace treaty (the Treaty of Aix-la-Chapelle) ended the War of the Austrian Succession in 1748. Under the terms of that treaty, Île Royale was returned to France. Louisbourg was reoccupied by the French during the summer of 1749. That same summer, the British established Halifax as a counterbalance to the French stronghold.

Left to right: The invasion fleet, the siege positions, and the bombarded town of Louisbourg.

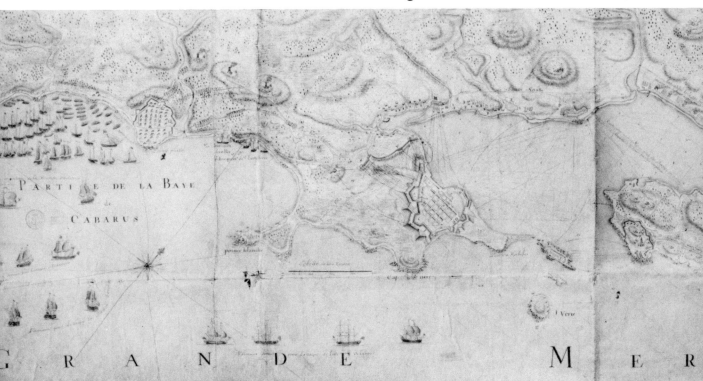

BACKGROUND TO THE 1758 SIEGE

The second siege of Louisbourg occurred during a
worldwide conflict known as the Seven Years' War. In
1756, Great Britain and France formally declared war
on each other again. In North America, however, the
hostilities had begun two years earlier. Then, in 1755,
the British had captured Fort Beauséjour, and the
Deportation of the Acadians (*le grand dérangement*)
had begun.

The formal outbreak of war in 1756 coincided with an
important change in the British government. William
Pitt took over as prime minister, and he adopted an
aggressive policy towards winning a decisive victory
in North America.

The first enemy efforts against Louisbourg were
British blockades off the coast. These did not cripple
the colony, but they did disrupt commercial, fishing,
and naval traffic to and from the port. The British then

attempted an assault on Louisbourg in 1757, but the attacking fleet arrived late and was eventually dispersed by a storm.

THE DEFENDERS

The beginning of the second siege saw the French in a far stronger position than in the first. There were approximately 3 500 soldiers and militia under the command of Governor Augustin de Boschenry Drucour. There was also strong naval support: six vessels of at least 50 cannons and four vessels with fewer than 50 cannons.

Although the general weaknesses of the fortifications remained, the damage suffered in 1745 had been repaired. Moreover, there were defensive positions along the coast, including a battery at Lighthouse Point, across the harbour from the fortress. A large number of Micmacs, allies to the French, were also at Louisbourg in 1758, which had not been the case in 1745.

THE ATTACKERS

The British attacking force of 1758 was much larger than the British-New England force of 1745. In fact, the combined army and naval force numbered approximately 27 000 men. Of that total, more than 13 000 troops were under the command of Major-General Jeffery Amherst. The naval support consisted of 23 vessels with at least 50 guns, and 11 warships with fewer guns. There were also smaller vessels and transports. This contingent of the Royal Navy was under the command of Admiral Edward Boscawen.

SIEGE EVENTS

When the British fleet arrived in Gabarus Bay, the weather conditions were not right to attempt a landing. For six days, the ships waited offshore, with every move being watched by the French defenders at Kennington Cove. Finally, on June 8, 1758, the British tried to come ashore. Just when the French thought they had beaten them back, several boats landed in rough surf along a stretch of shore that was out of sight. The British surprised the nearest defenders, attacking from an unexpected angle. The French in the immediate vicinity fled, and the other French positions soon gave way as well. Once the French had withdrawn to the fortress, the British landed the rest of their forces and built siege camps.

Between June 9 and June 18, the British established camps and began formal siege procedures (digging trenches and building batteries) against the town. Unlike 1745, in 1758 one of the first priorities was to silence the Island Battery. The British took over Lighthouse Point, erected their own battery there, and began bombarding the Island Battery. After a week of enduring bombardment, the French gave up the Island Battery, but they countered by scuttling four warships at the harbour entrance in an attempt to prevent the British vessels from entering the port.

The British then turned their attention to the main fortifications of Louisbourg. The bombardments were aimed at the Dauphin Gate area, which suffered heavy damage. A French frigate anchored in the harbour, the *Aréthuse,* was initially able to use its cannons to hinder British operations, but eventually it had to withdraw. On July 15, the *Aréthuse* escaped, eluding the blockade and sailing back to France.

The British intensified their attack on the remaining French ships. On July 21, a shell struck one of the French vessels, starting a fire that quickly destroyed three other ships. The following day, the King's Bastion barracks were hit, and burned. On July 25, the British succeeded in burning and capturing the last two French ships. At the same time, the attacking batteries were opening great holes in the walls. The French bowed to the inevitable, and on July 26, the Louisbourg garrison surrendered unconditionally.

The mid-point of the 1758 siege, with the town under bombardment and the major French ships still not captured or burned.

THE SIEGES—CONCLUSIONS

In both 1745 and 1758, the deciding factor was the superior strength of the attackers' naval and land forces. Like any fortified town, Louisbourg could hold out for only a limited amount of time. It would eventually fall to a larger besieging force unless relief arrived, but the nearest source of French supplies or reinforcements was too far away. This distance, together with British naval strength, sealed the fate of the fortress.

French plan detailing the stages of the 1758 siege.

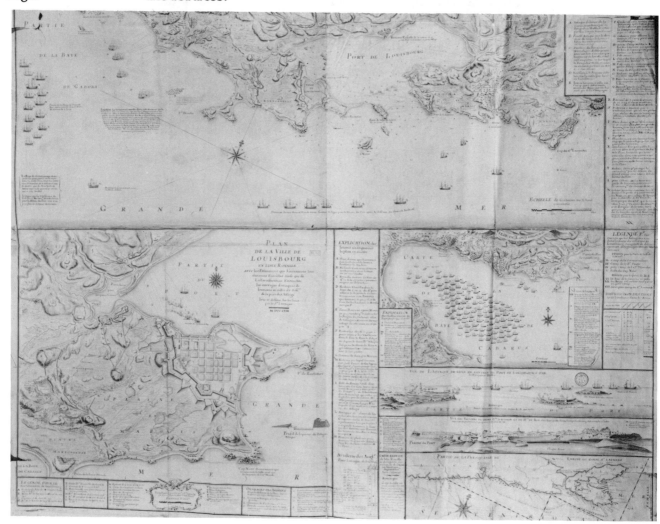

DID YOU KNOW?

Until 1752, France and Great Britain used different calendars. Both had the same 12 months, but the British one, known as the Julian calendar, did not accurately reflect the solar year. By the 18th century, the Julian calendar had fallen 11 days behind "real" astronomical time. The French calendar, on the other hand, was known as the Gregorian calendar—the same calendar used today, with 365-1/4 days a year. The addition of an extra day in February every four years—the "leap" year—makes the Gregorian calendar more accurate.

The differences between the two calendars meant that the events of the 1745 siege took place on different dates.

	British (Julian)	French (Gregorian)
Besiegers come ashore	April 30	May 11
Capture of Royal Battery	May 3	May 14
Surrender terms signed	June 16	June 27
British take possession	June 17	June 28

When Britain switched to the Gregorian calendar in 1752, there was a great public debate in the country over whether that calendar should be adopted. Some people protested that by moving the calendar ahead, the government was cheating them out of 11 days of their lives. Do you think they were right?

By the 1758 siege, the British and the French were using the same calendar.

SUGGESTED ACTIVITIES

1. Pick one of the two sieges, 1745 or 1758. Write an account of it as if you were a journalist on the scene. Make sure you answer the basic questions a journalist asks: who?, what?, when?, where?, why?

2. Design two posters, one that celebrates the capture of Louisbourg by the British, then one that laments the loss of the fortress by its French defenders.

THE MI'KMAQ

The Mi'kmaq are Nova Scotia's aboriginal people. They were living in the region even before the European explorers and colonists arrived. In fact, the Mi'kmaq are thought to have settled in what is now Atlantic Canada about 3 000 years ago.

The Europeans brought diseases to which the native people had no immunity, and many Mi'kmaq died as a result. The Mi'kmaq population before the arrival of the Europeans is unknown. In 1611, a French Jesuit estimated that there were 3 000-3 500 Mi'kmaq in the Maritimes, but this was after many had already died.

Although their population was relatively small by European terms, the Mi'kmaq inhabited a large area. Their traditional homeland included all of what is now Nova Scotia and Prince Edward Island, the eastern half of New Brunswick, and the Gaspé Peninsula of Québec. They also made visits to Newfoundland and voyages to the Magdalen Islands, to hunt seals and walrus.

MI'KMAQ ON ÎLE ROYALE

When the French settled on Île Royale in 1713, there were between 25 and 30 Mi'kmaq families living on the island. Other Mi'kmaq arrived from the mainland over the next few years, adding to the population. The total Mi'kmaq population on the island during the Île Royale period (1713-58) was probably about 250.

The Mi'kmaq moved from place to place to take advantage of different food sources. The French hoped to encourage the Île Royale Mi'kmaq to settle in one location. First, they wanted them to settle at a mission built at Mirliguèche, not far from the present-day community of St. Peters. Later, the mission was located at Île de la Ste.-Famille (Chapel Island).

Mi'kmaq-French contact occurred mainly at the missions in the southeastern part of the Bras d'Or Lakes—as the French had hoped—yet the Mi'kmaq never completely abandoned their traditional lifestyle. Occasionally, Mi'kmaq representatives visited Louisbourg, and once a year, French leaders went to Port Toulouse (St. Peters) to meet with the Mi'kmaq.

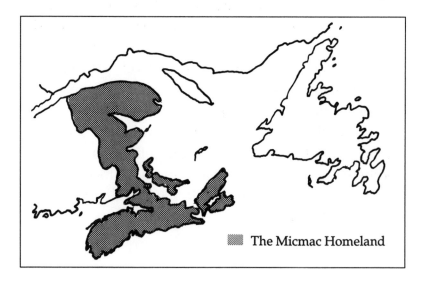

The Micmac Homeland

LIFE AMONG THE MI'KMAQ

The Mi'kmaq of two and three centuries ago survived off the land. Today, such a lifestyle may be considered harsh, but to the Mi'kmaq then, it was normal.

From birth, Mi'kmaq boys and girls learned the skills of survival—how to hunt and fish, cook, build shelters, and make clothing, which they decorated with intricate quillwork. Indeed, Mi'kmaq designs with porcupine quills are greatly admired today.

Detail from a Lewis Parker painting of traditional Mi'kmaq life.

The Mi'kmaq created beautiful designs.

The family was the basic social unit of the Mi'kmaq. A number of families usually grouped together to form a band. Each band occupied a particular area and had its own chief who co-ordinated activities and settled minor disputes. Serious crimes and major decisions were decided by the band elders. On Île Royale, there was only one band.

Occasionally, different bands came together for religious gatherings or to renew alliances or to wage

Detail from a painting by Lewis Parker.

war on a common enemy. In times of war, leaders were selected according to their reputation as warriors.

ALLIES TO THE FRENCH

French explorers and settlers attempted to form alliances with the native peoples they met in the New World. Such friendships helped them to survive in the strange new land. Native men also made excellent warriors, and France was eager to have them on its side in its fight against Britain.

Mi'kmaq warrior

When the French colonized Île Royale, they made sure they formed a strong bond with the island's Mi'kmaq. Missionaries played an important role in maintaining this alliance, and by the 18th century, many native people had been converted to the Roman Catholic faith.

A second reason for good French-Mi'kmaq relations was that the French treated the natives with respect. They regarded them as important allies, not as subservient people. For their part, the Mi'kmaq were careful not to be drawn into a subordinate position.

Each year the alliance between the French and the Mi'kmaq was renewed in formal ceremonies. The events took place between June and August at Port Toulouse, Port Dauphin (Englishtown), or Port Lajoie (Charlottetown, P.E.I.). The ceremonies involved native chiefs and French officials, with each side pledging friendship and aid to the other. The French hosted a feast for several hundred Mi'kmaq of all ages. After the feast, the French presented gifts of blankets, tools, muskets, bullets, and gunpowder.

WARTIME ACTIVITIES

To the French, the Mi'kmaq were most valuable as military allies, and officials at Louisbourg made every effort to maintain this alliance. During wartime, they encouraged the Mi'kmaq to attack British soldiers and settlers on mainland Nova Scotia. Missionaries often carried the French requests for assistance to the chiefs of the bands.

Mi'kmaq used warfare to seek redress for their own grievances against the British. These initiatives sometimes upset the diplomatic efforts of the French. Whether fighting for their own interests or on behalf of the French, the Mi'kmaq were often successful in their military efforts.

European soldiers, French or British, were not used to the forest warfare practised by North American Indians. Instead, they were used to pitched battles on open fields or lengthy sieges of fortified towns. Surprise Mi'kmaq guerilla attacks and ambushes tended to catch the European soldiers off guard and gave an advantage to native warriors.

In addition to their military success on land, the Mi'kmaq were also skilled in handling canoes and other boats. They were even known to capture New England schooners and then cruise the coast in them.

In 1744, Mi'kmaq warriors took part in two attacks on Annapolis Royal. In 1745, they assisted in another assault on that British fort. In 1758, Mi'kmaq then helped the French prevent the British from coming ashore at the beginning of the second siege of Louisbourg.

AFTERMATH

Following the capture of Louisbourg in 1758, the Mi'kmaq on Île Royale (renamed Cape Breton Island about this time) made peace overtures to the British officials. The chief of the island Mi'kmaq was one of a number of band leaders who signed treaties with the British at Halifax in 1760-61. During the early 1760s, the Mi'kmaq initiated contact with the French on St. Pierre and Miquelon. Although this annoyed British officials, many Mi'kmaq moved from Cape Breton Island to Newfoundland at this time.

SUGGESTED ACTIVITIES

1. Find out about the native people living closest to your community. Compare how they lived in the 18th century with how they live today.

2. Native arts and crafts are popular around the world. Pick a craft or an art form that appeals to you, then try your hand at it. If you can, get in touch with a local specialist who can teach you one of his or her crafts.

THE FISHERY

To a large degree, Louisbourg owed its existence to codfish. Of course, other factors led to the founding of the town, but the most important certainly had to do with the schools of millions of codfish that swam in the waters off 18th-century Île Royale. The fishery was in fact the heart of the Île Royale economy. There were far more people employed in fishery occupations—both in the boats and on shore—than there were in military or domestic positions.

bourg

EARLY USE & SETTLEMENT

Before the French arrived at Louisbourg, its anchorage had been known as English Harbour (Havre à l'Anglois). Indeed, since the 1500s the port had been an occasional base for British and other European fishermen. None of those early fishermen, however, had established a permanent settlement.

The French founded Louisbourg in 1713 for two main reasons. First, the Treaty of Utrecht, signed that year to end the War of the Spanish Succession, deprived them of their Placentia, Newfoundland, fishing base. The fishermen, soldiers, and settlers of Placentia had to move somewhere, and Île Royale offered excellent opportunities for continuing the fishery.

Second, Louisbourg was considered the best harbour on Île Royale. It had a large port that did not freeze

Two types of barrels used in the fishery.

over in winter; it was easy to enter, exit, and defend; cod were plentiful; and there was ample space on shore for curing the fish.

Views of the port of Louisbourg: 1717 (top), 1731 (bottom).

THE NORTH ATLANTIC FISHERY

Although some food was produced locally in 18th-century Louisbourg (kitchen gardens produced vegetables and herbs), most supplies came from France, Canada,* New England, Acadia, and the West Indies. The one major exception was fish. There were many species of fish, as well as other kinds of seafood, that could be harvested from the ocean.

*"Canada" refers to the settlements along the St. Lawrence River, not the present-day country.

Haddock and halibut, salmon and sole, lobsters and oysters—these were some of the species enjoyed by the people of Louisbourg. Yet the undisputed king of the ocean in the 18th century was cod.

Tens of thousands of Europeans came seasonally to the North Atlantic fishing banks in search of cod. Once dried or salted, cod fed millions more in Europe and the West Indies.

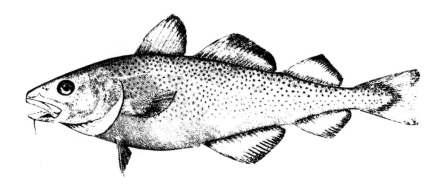

Fisherman splitting cod after the fish have been "headed" and "gutted."

THE IMPORTANCE OF COD

People have always needed to preserve food in some way, as fresh food has to be consumed quickly before it decays.

Many centuries ago, people discovered that they could prolong the "life" of certain foods by drying, smoking, or salting them. This was true for both meat and fish.

One of the most important commodities in the 18th century was dried or salted codfish. The abundant fish offered an excellent source of protein and had good preservative qualities. Dried cod was also easily transported. Moreover, meatless days on the church calendar created a steady demand for the preserved fish.

Dry fishery

TWO TYPES OF COD FISHERY

There were two ways to process and preserve cod. One was known as the "wet," or "green," fishery; the other as the "dry" fishery.

In the "wet" fishery, large ships sailed from France to the vast cod banks off Newfoundland and Île Royale. (The ships and crews went ashore only if necessary, for refit or for supplies.) Soon after the crews hauled the cod on board, they salted it. The salt cod was never taken ashore but was transported directly to France.

The "dry" fishery, on the other hand, required shore establishments where the drying process could take place. The drying was achieved by splitting the cod, then placing it on wooden "flakes," or racks. Through exposure to the sun and wind, and regular turning, the cod gradually lost its moisture. Some salt was also used, though much less than in the wet fishery. Once dried, the cod was ready for shipment to European or West Indian markets.

Wet fishery

FISHING VESSELS

Fishermen used different types of vessels, depending on the type of fishery in which they were involved.

For the offshore wet fishery, a relatively large ship called a *bateau* was commonly used. This vessel could hold a large quantity of cod, which was salted and then carried to France, where it was marketed.

Two vessels were commonly used in the dry fishery. One boat was known as a *chaloupe* (shallop). This small, undecked rowboat was equipped with a short mast. Shallops ranged from 5 to 10 metres in length and carried three-man crews. Used mainly in the inshore fishery, shallops took the cod ashore daily, so these boats did not need a large carrying capacity.

Part of the offshore fishing fleet.

The other vessel used in the dry fishery was the *goélette* (schooner). Schooners were larger than shallops, ranging from 17 to 25 metres in length. They had a carrying capacity of between 50 and 120 metric tonnes and held 11-man crews. Fishermen used schooners to fish on the banks, 30 kilometres or more offshore. They would stay on the banks for several days, then return to port with their catch.

A typical shore establishment.

SUGGESTED ACTIVITIES

1. Find out how many species of cod are in the ocean. List them and indicate their differences.

2. Atlantic Canada still has one of the world's great fisheries. Yet there are problems facing today's fishery that did not exist 200 years ago. Find out more about today's fishery, and compare fisheries past and present. If possible, visit a modern fish plant.

TRADE & COMMERCE

Louisbourg was once a major centre of trade and commerce in North America. For about half a century, from its founding in 1713 until its fall in 1758, the Île Royale port was one of the busiest along the Atlantic seaboard. Ships from France, the West Indies, New England, Acadia, and other parts of New France called regularly.

TRADE—THE BUYING & SELLING OF COMMODITIES

Louisbourg's trade was based on the export of dried cod. The preserved fish was one of the staples of life for many people in Europe and the West Indies. Demand was high, and prices were firm.

When merchant ships from France and the West Indies arrived in Louisbourg to purchase cod, they came with cargoes of European and West Indian products. These goods were unloaded at Louisbourg and sold to local merchants. The commodities were then purchased by the people of Louisbourg or resold by merchants and shipped to another market. This

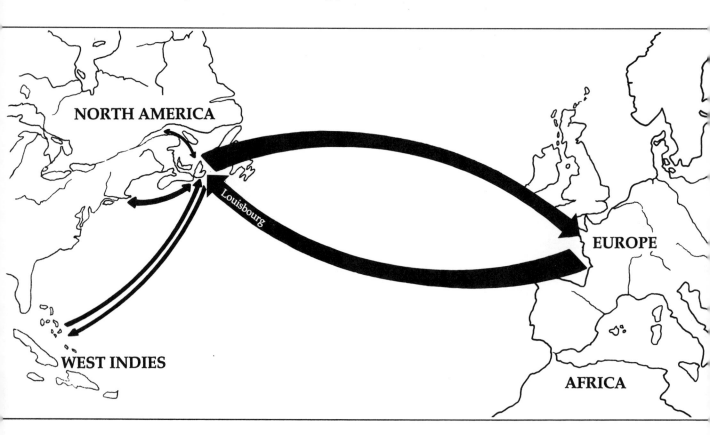

practice is known as transshipment. Louisbourg became an important "transshipment" centre for European and West Indian products. Merchants from New England, Acadia, and Canada came to purchase commodities for resale. This pattern of trade is often referred to as a "triangular" flow of goods.

Merchants made deals on the waterfront of every busy seaport.

LE PARFAI NEGOCIAN

LOUISBOURG TRADE

Much of the trade in 18th-century North America was carried out by ships. By the 1740s, an average of 130 to 150 ships sailed into Louisbourg every year. These were mostly fishing and trading vessels, along with a few warships. After anchoring, the trading vessels sold their cargoes, exchanged commodities, or delivered civilian or military supplies that had been ordered. Louisbourg had become a major port—a trading centre.

The busiest area at Louisbourg was the waterfront. There were five main wharves in the harbour and many warehouses nearby, in the town. A broad expanse of land between the water's edge and the first houses was known as the quay. (There were many houses and fish flakes on the waterfront outside the fortified town, and property lines were carefully observed.)

The King's Storehouse, Louisbourg.

Louisbourg's quay was busy with merchants making deals and people moving goods back and forth.

The busy port of Rochefort, France.

The coming and going of boats and barges and the hustle and bustle of people made the waterfront exciting. Sometimes auctions were held as well. During the summer shipping season, one could hear many different languages and accents along the quay. Breton, Basque, and Norman fishermen, English traders, West Indian merchants, and Acadian customers all contributed to the cosmopolitan feel of the seaport.

The quay was in many ways the heart of Louisbourg. It was here that goods came ashore, exports were readied for other destinations, and business deals were struck. It was also where wrongdoers were punished, such as in a public flogging or branding.

COINS OF THE REALM

When the people of Louisbourg spoke of how much something cost, they usually talked in terms of *livres*. The *livre* was the basic monetary unit, as the dollar is today.

A pair of shoes may have cost 1 *livre*, a jacket may have cost 10 *livres*, a servant may have made 40 or 50 *livres* for a year's work.

Although the *livre* was the basic monetary unit, there was no coin worth exactly one livre. Instead, there were some coins worth several *livres* and others worth less than one.

The smallest value in the 18th-century French monetary system was the *denier*. Then came the *sol* and the *livre*. Higher-value coins included the *écu* and the *louis d'or*. The money was worth the following:

12 *deniers* = 1 *sol*
20 *sols* = 1 *livre*
6 *livres* 12 *sols* = 1 *écu*
24 *livres* = 1 *louis d'or*

The least-valuable coins were made of copper or copper alloys; the more valuable were made of silver and gold.

HOW THINGS WERE PURCHASED IN THE 18TH CENTURY

When people buy something today, they usually pay cash, write a cheque, or use a credit card. In 18th-century Louisbourg, the methods of payment were slightly different. When people paid cash, they used only coins, as no paper money existed. They also used a barter system in which one good or service was exchanged for another good or service. For instance, a person may have offered a quantity of fish in return for vegetables worth the same amount. Merchants used letters of exchange, similar to cheques or promissory notes, where a buyer put in writing his obligation to pay for certain goods.

ILLEGAL TRADE

In addition to legitimate trade, Louisbourg's merchants sometimes carried on a secret, illegal trade with New England. To understand why such trade was illegal, one must understand how the economy was supposed to work in the 18th century.

Generally, nations in the 18th century did not want their colonies to trade with anyone but themselves. Countries strived to have a more or less self-contained trading system, dominating each of their colonies. This economic theory was known as mercantilism, and it was practised by both Great Britain and France.

The colony of Île Royale, therefore, was supposed to trade only with France and other parts of New France. In practice, French colonial officials recognized that Louisbourg sometimes had to buy supplies and provisions from New England. When food supplies ran low, or building materials were required quickly at low cost, some purchases had to be made in New England. As a result, New England cattle, pork, boards, bricks, and shingles regularly made their way to Louisbourg.

The New England trade with the French on Île Royale had strong opponents on the British side. Authorities claimed that it took away business from legitimate British or New England traders.

French merchants, on the other hand, claimed that Louisbourg's trade with New England was taking away their own chances for profit. Each time a New

England ship traded beef, pork, tobacco, tar, or textiles at the fortress town, it meant one less sale for a French merchant. Nevertheless, trade with New England flourished throughout the early 18th century, for Île Royale sometimes had no other source for certain foods and building supplies.

TRADE & COMMERCE WORD FIND

Look for the following words, spelled horizontally or vertically: cargo, commodity, cosmopolitan, hold, mercantilism, port, quay, staple.

W	G	H	J	K	L	P	O	T	R	F	H	J	S	T	R	C
O	Y	O	A	A	S	O	G	X	Z	Z	N	M	L	O	P	O
E	R	L	S	S	H	R	P	W	C	A	R	G	O	Q	Q	S
N	J	D	L	K	F	T	D	D	E	R	T	Y	Y	U	I	M
A	S	D	F	G	H	J	K	L	Z	X	C	V	B	N	M	O
M	E	R	C	A	N	T	I	L	I	S	M	T	U	S	B	P
A	F	R	T	Y	Q	A	S	O	I	P	T	Y	B	F	D	O
Q	S	D	F	G	H	J	K	L	Q	W	R	S	T	Y	U	L
U	Z	X	Z	X	G	H	M	N	V	A	S	E	I	I	O	I
A	D	G	S	T	A	P	L	E	Y	T	E	R	Y	U	I	T
Y	O	I	U	Y	T	R	E	W	Q	Q	W	E	R	T	Y	A
T	Y	Q	C	O	M	M	O	D	I	T	Y	A	A	T	S	N

ANSWERS TO TRADE & COMMERCE WORD FIND

```
W  G  H  J  K  L  P  O  T  R  F  H  J  S  T  R  C
O  Y  O  A  A  S  O  G  X  Z  Z  N  M  L  O  P  O
E  R  L  S  S  H  R  P  W  C  A  R  G  O  Q  Q  S
N  J  D  L  K  F  T  D  D  E  R  T  Y  Y  U  I  M
A  S  D  F  G  H  J  K  L  Z  X  C  V  B  N  M  O
M  E  R  C  A  N  T  I  L  I  S  M  T  U  S  B  P
A  F  R  T  Y  Q  A  S  O  I  P  T  Y  B  F  D  O
Q  S  D  F  G  H  J  K  L  Q  W  R  S  T  Y  U  L
U  Z  X  Z  X  G  H  M  N  V  A  S  E  I  I  O  I
A  D  G  S  T  A  P  L  E  Y  T  E  R  Y  U  I  T
Y  O  I  U  Y  T  R  E  W  Q  Q  W  E  R  T  Y  A
T  Y  Q  C  O  M  M  O  D  I  T  Y  A  A  T  S  N
```

THE NAVAL PORT

If you had to pick one reason for Louisbourg's importance in the 18th century, it would be its harbour. For before Louisbourg was anything else —a fortress or a community—it was a port.

THE PORT OF LOUISBOURG

As a port, Louisbourg had many advantages. The harbour was large enough to hold all the ships that needed to anchor there, and its narrow channel opening meant that shore batteries could easily defend it against enemy ships that tried to enter.

At that time, there was no precise way of determining longitude, so ships sailed across the ocean using the line of latitude that led directly from French ports such as Rochefort and La Rochelle to Louisbourg.

Finally, because Louisbourg was located on the eastern tip of Île Royale, which jutted out into the Atlantic, the port was ideally located for triangular trade routes to and from France, the West Indies, and the settlements along the St. Lawrence River.

THE DEVELOPMENT OF LOUISBOURG

The size and location of Louisbourg harbour, along with its proximity to the fishing banks, prompted the French to make Louisbourg the major settlement on Île Royale.

Once Louisbourg began to grow and prosper, French officials decided to make it the administrative centre, or capital, of the colony as well. In 1719, work began on the fortifications, which would eventually make the town one of the most formidable fortresses on the continent. Strong defences, together with the excellent harbour, turned Louisbourg into an important naval port.

Louisbourg harbour was spacious and well protected.

THE PIRATE THREAT

During the early 18th century, Île Royale commerce suffered pirate attacks. Pirates took anything of value: boats, supplies, fish oil. So serious were these menaces in the 1720s that the Governor feared that the town itself might be attacked. He readied the soldiers and had additional cannons mounted just in case. Luckily, the attack never came.

Most pirates were outlaws from English or French fishing vessels. Some had been dismissed from their ships for insubordination or drunkenness; others had deserted because of low wages and poor food. Often, men stole boats and gear from their masters to begin their career in piracy. In Louisbourg, a boat was taken from immediately below the windows of the financial administrator's residence, right on the waterfront.

One pirate headquarters was at Cape Ray, Newfoundland. In general, pirates were feared most for their raids on fishing vessels on the Grand Banks or along the Newfoundland coast.

LOUISBOURG—THE NAVAL PORT

As a busy port, Louisbourg had many onshore facilities. These included wharves and warehouses, inns and cabarets, Canada's first lighthouse (lit in 1734), a careening wharf to repair ships, and a hospital for sailors. There was even a special court that dealt specifically with maritime laws and regulations. Interestingly enough, all but one of Louisbourg's governors had been ship captains or naval officers at some time during their careers.

The port required many specialists. In addition to sailors, Louisbourg needed a port captain, pilots, navigators, clerks, and scribes. There was a hydrographer, who drew navigational charts, and even an astronomer for a few years. The astronomer's study of the stars was part of the worldwide attempt in the mid-18th century to find an accurate way of measuring longitude. In fact, Canada's first observatory was built at Louisbourg!

Louisbourg was a busy port right from the beginning.

NAVIGATIONAL AIDS & OTHER SIGNALS

All ports needed navigational aids. Along Île Royale's east coast, which could be foggy and stormy, that need was especially strong.

The most important navigational aid at Louisbourg was the lighthouse. Its light was produced by burning fish oil, and under perfect conditions, the Louisbourg light could be seen from as far as 3 leagues (12 kilometres) out at sea. In foggy weather, however, the lighthouse was of little use. On foggy days, signal guns were fired on shore to warn ships of the approaching coastline.

Flags were also used as signals. A large white flag indicated that Louisbourg was a French possession. A red flag warned that drift ice was inside the harbour and along the shore. A yellow flag signalled that the town and harbour were under quarantine.

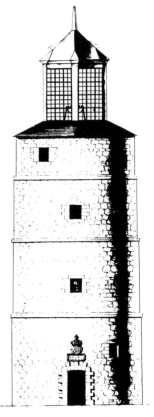

Louisbourg lighthouse

As well, markers, in the shape of crosses, were raised around the harbour mouth to help fishermen and sailors take their bearings.

ABOARD SHIP

Life aboard a large 18th-century ship was like that in a small village. Besides sailors, there were blacksmiths, sail-makers, clerks, cooks, a surgeon, coopers, cannoneers, and even soldiers.

As mentioned earlier, the cost of outfitting a large 18th-century warship for a six-month cruise was approximately equal to the annual expenditure on the fortifications of Louisbourg.

AN EXPOSED LANDWARD SIDE

When the French engineers designed the defences for Louisbourg, they worried most about an attack from the sea. As a result, the harbour was so well defended that it was practically impenetrable.

The same engineers and other colonial officials believed that the rocky coastline and marshy terrain around Louisbourg would prevent attackers from landing down the coast and coming by land to besiege the town from behind. Just in case, the French built high masonry walls on the landward side but placed very little artillery there.

Louisbourg light with a navigational cross nearby.

As it turned out, the New Englanders in 1745 and the British in 1758 did concentrate their assaults on Louisbourg's weakest front, its landward side. The naval port was so strongly defended that the besiegers knew they could not break through there without first weakening the other defences.

THE END OF THE NAVAL PORT

After the 1758 siege, the people of Louisbourg were deported to France. Two years later, British soldiers demolished the fortifications, and by the fall of 1761, only houses remained. Throughout the rest of the 18th century, Louisbourg was home to only a few scattered families of fishermen. It was still a port but no longer a major naval port.

FOOD & DIET

A good way to learn about people is through the food they eat. This is true whether one is learning about present or past cultures.

The methods of preserving food have changed dramatically over the years. Centuries ago, people did not have refrigerators or means of rapid transportation, so they could not enjoy fresh fruit and vegetables year round.

Instead, most people in 18th-century Louisbourg had to "dry" or "salt" perishables. Spices also helped prevent foods from spoiling. Once dried, salted, or spiced, many foods could then be stored for use in the winter, when few trading ships arrived with new supplies.

For the people of Louisbourg, like all the peoples of Europe, bread was the single most important food in the diet. There were many kinds and many shapes. On average, one person consumed several pounds of bread a day. While they ate a lot of bread, the people of Louisbourg did not eat potatoes at all. The potato had not yet become a staple of European diets.

bourg

THE FOOD OF LOUISBOURG

As a fishing port, Louisbourg was fortunate to have access to fresh seafood year round. Cod was the most common species, though the colonists also enjoyed salmon, halibut, and other fish. As well, they caught trout in lakes and streams and eels along the coast. Some people ate lobster and other shellfish; others regarded such dishes as poor people's food.

Louisbourg had many gardens, and many residents kept chickens, goats, and pigs. Some supplemented their diets through hunting animals such as hare, lynx, moose, black bear, caribou, and seabirds.

Despite plentiful fish and game, there was not nearly enough food to feed all the inhabitants of Louisbourg. Most staples—meat, flour, eggs, butter, fruits, and vegetables—came by ship. Foods from Europe, the West Indies, New England, and elsewhere in New France made their way to every household.

Ordinary provisions usually came in barrels. Animals (cattle, pigs, and sheep) arrived "on the hoof" aboard ships. The slaughter then took place in the fall or early winter.

A typical Louisbourg kitchen contained foods from many places: butter and salt beef from Ireland, cheese from Holland and France, vegetables from New England, Acadia, and the French settlements along the St. Lawrence River. There was also molasses and sugar from the West Indies and flour and wine from France.

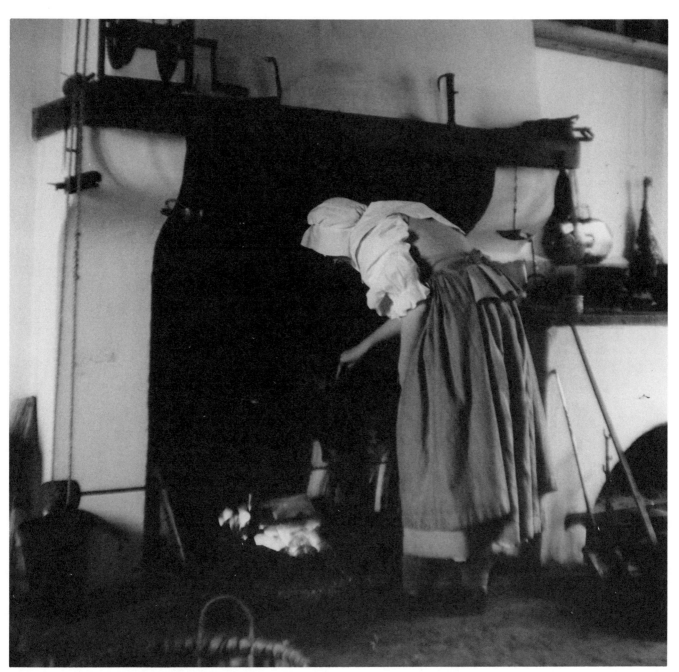

A typical Louisbourg kitchen.

FOOD IMPORTS TO LOUISBOURG

IMPORT	SOURCE	1737	1742	1743	1752
Salt Beef	France	yes	yes		
	Acadia		yes	yes	
	New England	yes	yes		yes
Cinnamon	West Indies	yes			
Chocolate	New England			yes	yes
	France	yes			yes
Pumpkin	New England		yes		
Preserves	France	yes			yes
	West Indies	yes			
Spices	France	yes			yes
Cheese	France	yes			yes
	New England		yes		yes

The above table indicates where a few of Louisbourg's imports came from, but only for selected years. In fact, there were many imports each and every year. Among the hundreds of commodities available were almonds and anchovies from France, apples, beans, and cabbages from New England, and liqueurs and olive oil from the French West Indies.

Louisbourg imported many kinds of cheese and some fruit.

The wine came from France, the rum from the West Indies.

BEVERAGES

People in the 18th century did not have the variety of beverages available today. Soft drinks, of course, did not exist. Fruit juices were rare and usually enjoyed only by the rich. Tea was difficult to obtain and expensive. Coffee and chocolate were more popular, yet even they were too expensive for poor people to buy on a regular basis. Coffee, in fact, was a relative novelty. The drink had been introduced in France in the mid-17th century.

Milk was not a common beverage. It was used primarily for cooking, though invalids and sick people also drank it. For infants, mother's milk was the most nutritious. Sometimes, however, goat's milk was a substitute.

One of the health problems that beset all early explorers and colonists was scurvy, a deficiency disease caused by a lack of vitamin C. People with scurvy felt weak and sore, their gums were extremely tender, and their breath was foul smelling. One way to prevent the illness among the soldiers at Louisbourg was to give them a ration of spruce beer, made from spruce twigs and molasses. This mild beer was also popular among the townspeople.

Spruce beer was a popular drink in the 18th century.

RECIPES

As a rule, 18th-century cooks did not rely on written recipes. Indeed, aside from professional chefs, most of them were not able to read. These everyday cooks had learned by watching their mothers or other cooks. They used their sense of taste, smell, and sight to tell them when a dish was ready.

The recipes that did exist were very different from today's. Instead of specific ingredients and precise quantities, there were simple general descriptions. It was not always clear how long a particular step should take. Of course, to 18th-century cooks, such precision was probably not necessary. They were familiar with the cooking techniques of the period. All they needed from a recipe was a general idea or maybe an unusual way to combine flavours. The following are two 18th-century dishes whose recipes have been adapted for present-day cooks.

FRENCH TOAST

This is a well-known treat but without the eggs.

4 to 6 thick slices bread
1 cup (250 mL) milk
Oil
Butter
1/4 cup (50 mL) sugar

Dip the bread in the milk. Lightly grease a pan with half oil and half butter. Heat to a moderate temperature. Fry the bread on both sides until heated through. Sprinkle with the sugar and place in a medium oven until golden.

EGGS WITH CANDIED CITRON PEEL

Eggs for dessert? Why not? Here's a sweet treat to go along with supper.

4 tbsp (60 mL) soft bread crumbs
1/4 cup (50 mL) milk or cream
5 eggs, well beaten
1/4 tsp (1 mL) salt (or to taste)
1 tsp (5 mL) sugar
2 tsp (10 mL) candied citron peel
1/4 tsp (1 mL) orange flower water
2 tbsp (25 mL) butter
Sprinkle of sugar

Soak the bread crumbs in milk for 15 to 20 minutes. Purée or strain through a fine sieve; add to the well-beaten eggs. Add the salt, 1 tsp (5 mL) sugar, citron peel, and orange flower water; mix well.

Melt the butter in a frying pan. When it begins to bubble, add the egg mixture. Stir gently until the liquid has evaporated and the eggs have reached the desired firmness. Sprinkle lightly with sugar and serve.

FIREPLACE EQUIPMENT

Cooking with a fireplace was much different than cooking with a modern stove or a microwave. First, one had to be a little stronger, as cast-iron pots and pans were very heavy, especially when filled with soup or stew. Second, one always needed a fire, even on the hottest days, and had to wait until the fire reached just the right intensity, then keep it there. In addition, one had to keep a constant eye on the pots on the fire, turning them regularly so that the heat spread evenly. Clearly, for a person today, cooking at a hearth would take some practice.

Here are some objects from a typical 18th-century kitchen. Identify them and explain their use.

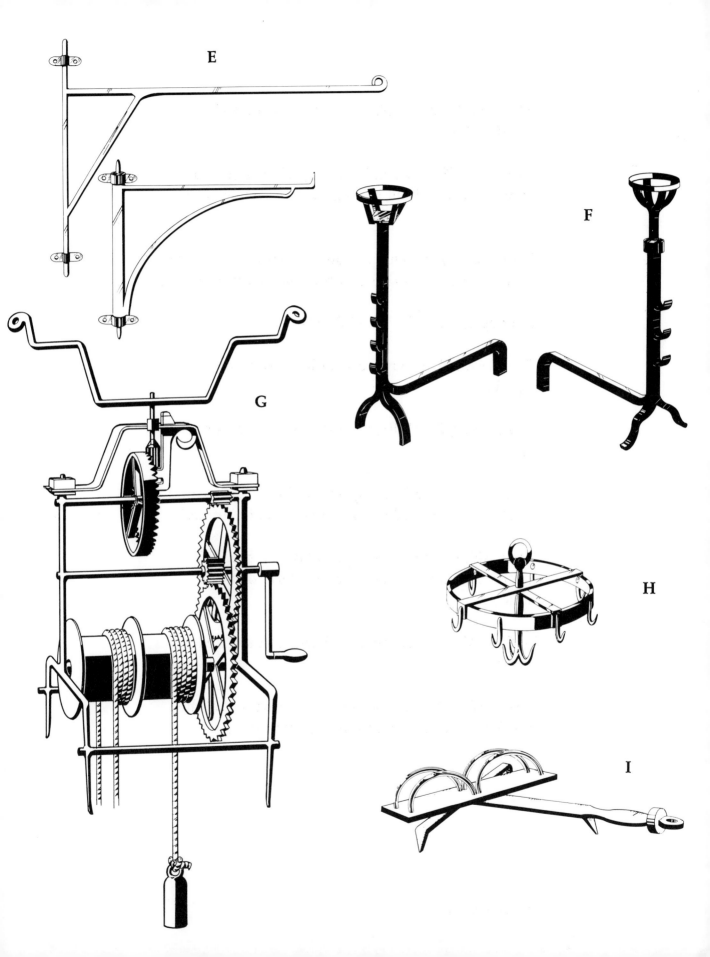

E

F

G

H

I

ANSWERS TO QUESTIONS ON FIREPLACE EQUIPMENT

A) POTAGER, or warming oven, where a cook kept things warm without having to have them on or near the fire.

B) BELLOWS, which one pumped with two hands to force air over a dying fire or hot coals, causing flames.

C) Long-handled FRYING PANS.

D) SKIMMER, which was a ladle for skimming liquids.

E) Swinging CRANES, used for hanging pots over a fire.

F) ANDIRONS, which supported the burning wood in a fire. The hooks held the metal rod of a turnspit.

G) TURNSPIT, for roasting meat over a fire. This mechanism gave 18th-century cooks a rotisserie option.

H) CROWN, for hanging fresh game or smoked meats.

I) TOASTER, whose slice holder turned so that the bread could be toasted evenly on both sides.

GARDENS

When the French arrived in Louisbourg, they
discovered that they could not grow everything they
wanted to. The area's acidic soil and short summer
were not suitable for growing the quantity and
variety of vegetables produced in France. Instead, the
colonists confined themselves to small kitchen
gardens known as *potagers*. Town plans show that
there were more than 100 such gardens within the
walls of the fortress where one could grow a range of
vegetables and herbs; flowers were much less
common.

Typical vegetables included cabbages, turnips,
carrots, beans, and peas. Cooks relied on herbs to give
flavour to soups, stews, and other dishes. They also
used some for medicinal purposes, such as to cure
headaches or to prevent upset stomachs. Mint,
parsley, sage, and thyme were common, and a few of
the herbs brought by Europeans now grow wild on
Cape Breton Island, including chives, caraway,
chicory, wild parsnips, and angelica.

Several gardens of Louisbourg were quite elaborate.
They had wide gravel paths and symmetrically
arranged beds. Sundials or urns often gave the
gardens a central focus. Through careful planning,
gardeners achieved attractive colour combinations.
They also put the sweetest-smelling plants along the
borders so that passers-by could enjoy the scent.

SUGGESTED ACTIVITIES

1. Louisbourg imported a lot of food, as do many present-day Atlantic communities. In any modern kitchen, one is likely to find meat from Alberta, oranges from Florida, canned pineapple from the Philippines, and much more.

   Make a list or a poster of the food your family eats and where it comes from. Read the labels on the cans and packages, and ask your grocer where he or she gets his or her fresh fruit and vegetables.

2. The gardens of Louisbourg had raised beds surrounded by fences or walls. These techniques helped to conserve moisture in the ground and to keep the garden area warmer. The gardens also featured symmetrical designs.

   Design an 18th-century garden. Pretend you are doing the design for a wealthy Louisbourg household. The owners would like a sundial or some other feature in the centre. Remember, the garden should be symmetrical and should contain mostly vegetables and herbs.

EDUCATION

Today, the law says that all children between the ages of 5 and 16 have to go to school.

Such a law seems normal, yet it is fairly recent. Until the mid-1800s, there were relatively few schools, and attendance was strictly a matter of choice. Most parents had neither the interest nor the money to send their children to school. Consequently, few children ever learned to read and write.

For generations, most people could only make a mark when asked to sign their name. To them, having the ability to write did not seem important. More pressing was learning a trade or a skill, to earn a living.

Louisbourg was not much different from the rest of colonial North America. Schools were difficult to establish, qualified teachers were hard to find, and students were few and far between.

Before the mid-1800s, education in many countries was mainly the responsibility of the church. In many

Ste. Marguerite Bourgeoys (1620-1700), foundress of the Sisters of
the Congregation of Notre-Dame.

towns or villages, as in Louisbourg, catechism classes—question-and-answer sessions on the articles of the Roman Catholic faith—formed the only schooling some children ever received. More formal schools, or even small colleges, were usually staffed by nuns or priests, and in general, the focus was more on religion than on the subjects taught today.

During the late 1700s, a debate raged across Europe over the kind of education children should receive. Some thought it was dangerous to give "ordinary" children too much education. They believed that once a child learned to read and write, he or she would no longer want to do manual jobs. They would then move from the farm to the cities in search of "easier" work. Others argued that society would improve only if more people received a good education, and this opinion prevailed. Today, virtually every country has compulsory education.

EDUCATION IN 18TH-CENTURY LOUISBOURG

In Louisbourg, despite its size, education was not a priority. In fact, Louisbourg may never have had a school if it were not for the Bishop of Québec. Bishop Saint-Vallier tried to convince the colonial administrators to do something about education, but they always refused. At last, in 1727, he took the matter into his own hands. He sent a teaching nun from the Congregation of Notre-Dame in Montréal to Louisbourg, to open a school for girls. Within two months of her arrival, there were 22 students enrolled in the school.

During the 1730s and 1740s, the number of teaching sisters ranged between three and six. At times, there may have been as many as 50 or 100 students.

For parents who wanted their sons to receive an education, there were two options: hire a local tutor or send the child to school in France or Québec. Obviously, only wealthy people could consider these options.

The girls who attended the Congregation of Notre-Dame's school at Louisbourg ranged in age from 6 to 18. The ideal student was "modest, docile and obedient." Children with communicable diseases could not attend, nor could girls who were engaged to be married.

The objective of the curriculum was to provide a Christian education. The program explained the fundamental articles of the Roman Catholic faith and promoted the virtues of piety and modesty. It taught reading and writing and gave practical instruction in needlework and other "female accomplishments."

There was no school on Sunday, when students had to attend church.

Students were always supervised. The following was a typical schoolday:

Breakfast, followed by a 15-minute study period.

8:30-9:00—Catechism class.

9:00-11:00—Class on a topic. The teacher read aloud from religious material, then asked the students questions.

Dinner—Silence was observed.

1:00-3:00—Reading, writing, and perhaps arithmetic.

3:00-3:30—Light snack.

3:30-4:30—Study period, followed by a reading on the life of one of the saints.

4:30—Day students went home, boarders had a half-hour free time.

5:00-6:00—Prayers and catechism.

6:00—Supper, followed by 2 to 2-1/2 hours of free time for recreation.

There were two kinds of students: those who boarded at the Congregation of Notre-Dame's school and those who attended only daytime classes and returned home in the afternoon.

The schoolweek ran from Monday to Saturday, with the same daily routine followed on Saturday, until 3:00 p.m. There was no schooling on Sunday, when attending Mass and Vespers and other religious obligations had to be met.

The school year was longer than it is today. There was almost no vacation during the fall, winter, and spring. The exception was January 1, when the students went home after Vespers. The only extended vacation was from August 15 to September 15.

SUGGESTED ACTIVITIES

1. Pretend you are a boarder or a daytime student at the Louisbourg school. Write an entry in your diary describing what you did today. Be sure to mention what you are studying and how the teacher treats you and the other children. How does it feel to be able to read and write when so many others cannot?

2. What is your view of compulsory public education? Has it been a beneficial or harmful development? Debate the topic with your classmates.

CLOTHING & FASHION

Every era has distinctive fashions, and the 18th century was no different. Just as today's world has regular changes in hair and clothing styles, so too did the world of 18th-century Louisbourg.

18TH-CENTURY FASHION

Louisbourg's fashions were set in France. What was popular to wear in the mother country eventually became stylish in the colony. Sometimes it took a few years for a particular fashion—say, a new dress or wig—to make its way across the Atlantic. Sooner or later, however, most colonists adopted the same look that was in vogue in France.

When one speaks of 18th-century fashions, one is really talking about the clothing and hairstyles of the well-to-do. Working people such as fishermen and servants did not keep up with fashions. Year in, year out, they wore the same basic garments. The clothes they could afford were usually hand-me-downs or purchases made at a local auction.

Wealthy and middle-income people, on the other hand, could afford to follow changing fashions. For these men, women, and children, it was important to maintain a stylish appearance.

CLOTHING STYLES

Fisherman

Fishermen were a familiar sight in 18th-century Louisbourg. They had to wear clothing that suited their work and the climate. Their *culottes* (trousers) were made of rugged, striped, hand-woven fabric and were cut in a straight-leg style. Decades later, the trousers lengthened and became the "bell-bottoms" associated with sailors.

The fisherman's vest was loose fitting so that he could move easily. His natural-linen shirt was coarse but very durable, and his woollen toque was practical for working at sea or along a windy shore. His thick hand-knit socks kept his feet warm, and his wooden shoes kept them drier than leather ones would have. The fisherman wore tarred canvas sleeves and an apron when handling fish.

Officer

As a military stronghold, Louisbourg always had many soldiers, as well as officers to lead them. The officer's uniform was made of finer material than that of an ordinary soldier's uniform. It was also more fashionably cut. Gold braid and buttons trimmed the pockets and sleeves. The *chemise* (shirt) was made of fine linen and was often trimmed with lace. Officers usually wore a *gorget* around their necks, a symbolic remnant of the armour once worn by knights. Wigs were common and stylish. One kind had side rolls with the back encased in a black silk bag tied with ribbon.

Louisbourg was also home to many families. There were hundreds of mothers and children who did not come from wealthy backgrounds. Some women were servants; others were widows who took in boarders, or seamstresses who made other people's clothes. The garments of these working women were well worn. They bought only what they could afford, usually items purchased at auctions. Colour co-ordination was the least of their worries. Most children wore make-overs or hand-me-downs.

The garments of working women and of children were well worn.

For the wealthy, it was important to maintain a stylish appearance.

Upper-class woman

There were far more "ordinary" women in Louisbourg than there were upper-class women who could afford fancy dresses. One of the stylish dresses was known as the *robe à la française*.

Drummer

Few people were more important in an 18th-century garrison town than the drummer. His drum calls throughout the day signalled activities. There was one drum call for the gates to open, another for them to close. Other beats announced drills or sentry changes.

The important role of the drummer meant he wore a colourful costume. He had to be the most easily recognized member of the military forces. His stockings, breeches, and vest were red. His *justaucorps* (jerkin) was blue and laced with the King's livery.

THE LOOK

Eighteenth-century clothes often had a free-flowing yet snug-fitting look. People thought such fashions made them appear elegant and refined. If they could afford to have their garments made with an expensive fabric such as silk, then so much the better. They believed that fabrics that shimmered made them look more dignified.

For fashion-conscious men, the ideal was to be clean-shaven, delicately perfumed, and wearing a powdered and curled wig.

FABRICS & DYES

There were no synthetic (manmade) fabrics in the 18th century—no nylon or rayon or polyester. Instead, all garments were made from natural fabrics—cotton, wool, linen, and silk. Tailors used these materials alone or in combination. All clothes were hand-sewn, sometimes by a local tailor or seamstress.

The colours of 18th-century garments came from natural vegetable dyes, which produced soft, subtle hues. When washed repeatedly or worn often in bright sunshine, however, the fabrics faded noticeably.

Fabric with floral pattern.

UPPER-CLASS MAKE-UP

In the 18th-century, it was fashionable for the upper classes to wear a lot of make-up. This was sometimes true for men, as well as for women.

In general, people who "painted" themselves wanted a white face with red cheeks and lips. They applied a white lead-base make-up, then added rouge to their cheeks. (The lead make-up, however, was often harmful, causing cancer.) They used beauty marks (patches cut from black velvet or silk) to hide blemishes and to highlight certain features. These patches were in the shape of a heart, square, tree, or anything the imagination could conjure. One woman wore as many as 15 patches at the same time. Some men also wore beauty marks.

One 18th-century gentleman is being shaved, while another is examining his face in a mirror.

Some high-ranking women preferred not to "paint" their faces. Maria Theresa of Spain, for instance, objected to applying so much make-up. Yet when she arrived at the court of France, the King informed her she must follow the fashion. She did as she was told.

One reason why beauty marks and heavy make-up became popular was that they covered blemishes. Smallpox and other diseases were common in the 18th century. Many people had disfigured or pock-marked faces, and they were glad to have ways to hide the blemishes.

SUGGESTED ACTIVITY

You are an 18th-century fashion designer. You have to design a new outfit for the Governor of Louisbourg or a new dress for his wife. Create one or the other, using your knowledge of 18th-century fashion.

INSIDE LOUISBOURG HOMES

It's easy to see from the outside that Louisbourg's houses were different from those in present-day towns and cities. But what were these 18th-century homes like inside?

Louisbourg waterfront buildings.

CROWDED LIVING CONDITIONS

Louisbourg, 1731

If people today could travel back in time to 18th-century Louisbourg, they may find one aspect of life annoying: the often-crowded living conditions.

Generally, 18th-century families were much larger than those today. Many parents had 6, 8, or even as many as 12 children. In-laws sometimes lived in the same house, and so did servants or slaves. Not only were families usually larger, but houses were typically smaller. (There were exceptions, of course, such as the chief engineer's residence.) The lack of central heating further reduced living space: many families did not use certain rooms once the weather turned cold.

Despite these crowded conditions, family life in Louisbourg was far from unbearable.

PARTITIONS & PRIVACY

One easy and inexpensive way to deal with crowded living conditions in 18th-century Louisbourg was to erect lightweight wooden partitions. These partitions could be put up quickly, then taken down when no longer needed. New, small rooms could be created in large, open spaces.

Such partitioned spaces offered a measure of privacy. But what was the acceptable level of privacy? Eighteenth-century standards were different from those today. The wooden partitions were not soundproof, and sometimes the curious could see through the cracks where the wood was joined.

The 18th-century family typically performed more functions than the present-day family. Besides providing food and shelter, adults were responsible for the education, religious training, and welfare of their children. There were also more family-run businesses than there are now. It is no exaggeration to say that the family unit was one of the mainstays of 18th-century society.

Partitions provided some privacy.

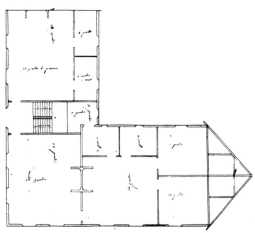

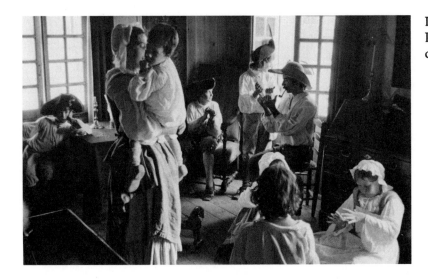

Living conditions in Louisbourg were crowded.

FLEXIBILITY IN HOME LIFE

Because of the relatively crowded conditions inside Louisbourg homes, it was necessary for people to be both organized and creative in their living arrangements. A flat-topped chest, for instance, could be a place to store things, a seat, or a table top.

With limited space, everything had to have its place. Thus, in at least one kitchen, there was a large table "under which there is a bed for a boy." Perhaps the boy slept there for the night, or perhaps the bed was pulled closer to the kitchen fire.

Mattresses that could be moved easily were another common feature. Filled with straw or feathers, they were all that many people had to sleep on. During the day, they were rolled up and put away; at night, they were unrolled and spread out. If lumpy straw-filled mattresses sound a bit uncomfortable, conditions were often worse in public houses. In many 18th-century European inns, overnight guests slept on straw-covered floors.

Another practical way of dealing with limited space was through the use of folding tables. Records show that one homeowner had no fewer than five such tables in his dining room. There were also chairs that could be stacked on top of each other and kept more or less out of the way. This could not be done with all chairs, but simply styled ones (without arms and with straw or cane seats) stacked easily. Another homeowner at Louisbourg had 14 straw chairs stored in a bedroom. Still another kept 18 straw chairs in his antechamber.

When it came to furnishings, necessity was often the mother of invention. Tapestries were hung on walls, used as carpets, table covers, and even heavy blankets. Of course, almost any fabric could serve as a blanket. One seaman used a heavy, lined cape. Another person used a thin mattress.

Chairs and mattresses could be stacked out of the way.

Whenever a desired furnishing was unavailable or too expensive, the people of Louisbourg had no choice but to find a creative solution.

WASTE NOT, WANT NOT

Today, we live in a "throw-away" society; that is, many things are quickly discarded after use.

In 18th-century Louisbourg, people did not throw things away. Goods came in simple—often reusable—containers and packages. Manufactured items were expensive, so few people could afford to discard them when they were damaged or broken. Instead, they repaired them whenever possible. Even the well-to-do found new uses for old furniture.

Archaeological excavations at Louisbourg reveal how common it was for residents to reuse various household wares. One bowl had been broken, then repaired with wire going through four pairs of holes drilled on either side of the break. A platter had six lead staples on either side of a large crack. The surface of the platter had been sanded to preserve its smooth appearance.

Other artifacts that had been adapted for reuse included bottle fragments ground down and turned into containers, and bits of broken porcelain for gaming pieces.

The reluctance to throw anything away touched every household in the 18th century. People lived by the proverb "waste not, want not."

KEEPING WARM

Imagine for a moment that it is a cold winter's night and you are living in a house without a furnace. That means there are no hot-water radiators and no hot-air vents. How do you keep warm?

In the 18th century, the most common source of heat was the fireplace. A fire can provide a lot of heat, but much of it goes up the chimney. And the farther one moves away from the fireplace, the cooler the air. So how did 18th-century people keep warm when far from a fireplace or in rooms without one?

At Louisbourg, brick stoves were common responses to the heating problem. Bricks were laid to form a boxlike structure—the stove—to which was attached an iron door, a top plate, and a stove pipe. Such stoves were temporary measures. They could be constructed each fall and taken apart the following spring. Stoves made entirely of iron were also used, yet they were more expensive to build than the brick ones.

One French visitor to 18th-century Canada commented that in spite of the colder climate, the widespread use of stoves in New France actually made living conditions warmer than they were in the mother country.

SUGGESTED ACTIVITY

Look around your home, your neighbourhood, and your school. Are there items or activities that an 18th-century person would find wasteful?

AN ASTRONOMICAL OBSERVATORY

In addition to playing an important role in Canadian history, Louisbourg played a part in Canadian science. The first astronomical observatory in what is now Canada was built at Louisbourg in 1750.

THE YOUNG ASTRONOMER & HIS ASSIGNMENT

In 1750, a 26-year-old French astronomer named Joseph-Bernard Chabert de Cogolin arrived at Louisbourg. He had been assigned to correct the maps of what is now Atlantic Canada. Chabert stayed at Louisbourg for only a year and a half, but in the course of that stay, he completed his task and also established what was the first observatory in the country.

Chabert de Cogolin was born in Toulon, on the Mediterranean coast of France, in 1724. He joined the navy in 1741, at the age of 17, and pursued a naval career, finally becoming a vice admiral in 1792.

Chabert de Cogolin's first voyage to New France was in 1746, when he was a navigator with the ill-fated

Gregorian telescope

D'Anville expedition. On his return to France in late 1746, the youthful Chabert de Cogolin reported that the charts of the North American coastline were not as accurate as they could have been. He proposed that he be assigned to make them more accurate. In 1750, the Minister of the Marine gave his approval for the young astronomer to travel back to the colonies to begin correcting French maps.

EQUIPMENT & ARRIVAL

To assist Chabert de Cogolin in his map work, the Ministry of the Marine provided him with a ship, an assistant, and a whole range of navigational and astronomical equipment. In total, he brought no fewer than eight telescopes. Six were refracting telescopes with focal lengths between one and six metres. Another was a Gregorian reflecting telescope with a focal length of about one metre. Other equipment included a seconds clock, terrestrial globes, maps of the stars, and an octant.

Mobile quadrant and other instruments

With his many instruments carefully stowed away, Chabert de Cogolin set sail from Brest in June 1750, aboard the frigate *La Mutine*. His assistant was the Chevalier de Diziers-Guyon, who was well known for his knowledge of geometry.

Soon after his arrival at Louisbourg, Chabert de Cogolin set up his astronomical instruments in the Governor's garden. This proved an unsatisfactory location, as he found "the intensity of the cold ... would not permit [him] to work in the open air." He felt he needed a specially built structure. As he was staying in the King's Bastion barracks, he decided to have a small building constructed that would serve as an observatory. Described as a "timber work cabin," the building was erected on the southern flank of the King's Bastion. A contractor carried out the "carpentry, joinery, locksmithing and glaziery."

WHY LOUISBOURG?

Why did Chabert de Cogolin establish an observatory at Louisbourg when that seaport had a reputation for foggy weather?

Although it is true that mountaintops are better places to build observatories than foggy coasts, Louisbourg was selected as the site for Chabert de Cogolin's observations because of its importance as a New World seaport. It was the first port of call for many French ships sailing to North America, so it was important that its geographic location be pinpointed as accurately as possible. In Chabert's own words,

Chabert de Cogolin

I have … to fix with exactitude the longitude of Louisbourg, both in order to facilitate the landing of vessels coming into that port and in order that in the drawing of maps one could start from this point in locating all others on the coast of this part of North America on their true meridians.

To supplement their Louisbourg observations, Chabert de Cogolin and Diziers-Guyon made voyages to other parts of the region. At each stop, they tried to determine the precise latitude and longitude.

CHABERT DE COGOLIN'S FINDINGS

For more than a year, Chabert de Cogolin and his assistant made astronomical observations at Louisbourg. In September 1751, they returned to France. Soon afterwards, Chabert de Cogolin began corresponding with many European astronomers to compare his Île Royale observations with those calculated at other locations. Of particular use were an English astronomer's findings taken at Greenwich, England.

Two years after Chabert de Cogolin's return to France, the French Royal Academy of Sciences published a report documenting his findings at Louisbourg. It was a sophisticated piece of work, and Chabert de Cogolin was commended for his contribution.

THE LOUISBOURG OBSERVATORY

Although the wooden observatory erected on the King's Bastion was built specifically for Chabert de Cogolin, it was not torn down after the astronomer returned to France. Nine months later, in June 1752, a Louisbourg engineer and accomplished cartographer, or map-maker, named Pierre Boucher used the structure. Other officials in town owned their own telescopes and likely used the observatory as well.

LATITUDE & LONGITUDE

While Chabert de Cogolin was at Louisbourg, he made many scientific observations. He noted details on the climate and the tides and on the stars and the moon. The main purpose of his stay, however, was to determine the exact longitude of the Île Royale capital. Indeed, cartographers and geographers in Europe and North America concluded that the young astronomer had accomplished what he had set out to do.

What is longitude? To help answer that question, look at a map.

Note first that there are lines running horizontally (that is, parallel to the Equator). These are lines of latitude measured in degrees, either north or south of the Equator. For example, Louisbourg is at about 46 degrees north latitude. Navigators in the mid-18th century were able to take latitude readings from the midday sun or the night-time stars by using instruments known as octants or sextants.

Now examine the lines running up and down the map, from the North Pole at the top to the South Pole at the bottom. These are lines of longitude. These lines begin from an imaginary line (like the Equator, at point zero) that passes through Greenwich, England. Every other line of longitude is defined by its relation to this Greenwich line; that is, it is a certain number of degrees to the east or the west of the baseline. Louisbourg, for example, is about 60 degrees west of Greenwich.

By finding where lines of latitude and longitude
intersect, one is able to locate any point on the surface
of the Earth, as no two positions can have the same
co-ordinates.

Back in the 1750s, however, scientists and navigators
had not yet figured out how to get accurate readings
of longitude. But seafaring nations such as England,
France, Holland, and Spain were eager to see the
longitude puzzle solved. Then ships' captains and
navigators would be able to tell more precisely their
location when sailing an east-west course. Large
rewards were offered to anyone who could devise a
reliable method of determining longitude. Joseph-
Bernard Chabert de Cogolin's stay in Louisbourg was
an attempt to solve this long-standing problem.

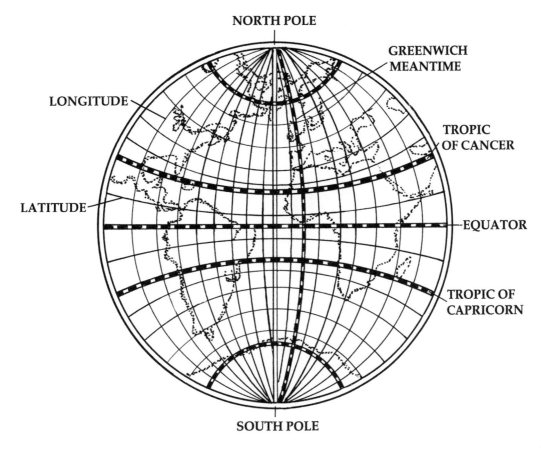

SUGGESTED ACTIVITIES

1. Find and compare the co-ordinates (latitude and longitude) of your hometown and four major world capitals.

2. What is a sundial and how does it work? Have you ever heard of a gnomon? Read about sundials in an encyclopedia, and then draw your own on cardboard or bristol board. Use a pencil or some other object as a gnomon. Experiment with it to see if you can get it to tell time accurately.

HEALTH & DISEASE

Health standards were much lower in the 18th century than they are today. One reason was that medical knowledge of how diseases and infections spread was not so advanced. Another was that standards of cleanliness were not so high. Also, 18th-century people faced diseases such as smallpox that are no longer threatening. Finally, the health-care system was not comprehensive.

CONTAGIOUS DISEASES

Seaport towns such as Louisbourg were especially susceptible to contagious diseases because they welcomed as many as 100 ships or more a year. It was not unusual for at least a few crew members on those ships to be suffering from disease. As Louisbourg was a centre for international trade, some sailors carried maladies picked up in Europe, the West Indies, or even the Far East.

The most deadly disease was dysentery. During the New England occupation of Louisbourg in 1745-46, more than 1 000 soldiers died from the "bloody fluxes." Then there was smallpox. Twice in the town's history, carriers of smallpox arrived in port. The first serious outbreak occurred in 1732-33. The death rate in the town tripled as a result, and many of the victims were children. In 1755, smallpox swept through Louisbourg again.

Fortunately, an effective smallpox vaccine began to be developed in the mid-18th century. According to the World Health Organization, smallpox was eliminated altogether by 1977.

Even when there was no smallpox at Louisbourg, other infectious diseases—or unsanitary practices— led to a high death rate among young people. Approximately one of every five children born there died before they reached the age of 12. But even that mortality rate was not so high as it was in 18th-century Europe. In France, it was generally accepted that one-quarter of all infants would die before they turned one.

PRECAUTIONS AGAINST EPIDEMICS

Health care was not advanced in the 18th century.

In an attempt to prevent the spread of contagious diseases at Louisbourg, port officials inspected ships arriving from places where smallpox and other diseases were known to be a problem. When such a disease reached Louisbourg, steps were taken to isolate those afflicted so that others would not be put at risk. As a routine measure, all ships had to report on the health of their passengers and crew.

Besides dysentery in 1745-46 and smallpox in 1732-33 and 1755, there was an outbreak of typhus in 1757. There was even one death from yellow fever, a disease commonly found in the tropics.

Generally, people who died from contagious diseases were not buried in the town cemetery but in emergency burial grounds dug outside the walls.

COMMON AILMENTS

Common ailments such as the cold and influenza also existed in the 18th century. Other typical maladies included dental problems, abscesses, and ulcers. Wealthy Louisbourg residents sometimes travelled to France to "take the waters" at mineral springs to improve their health. As the climate on Île Royale was damper and colder than in France, many blamed their respiratory problems and rheumatism on the long winters.

SANITATION & PERSONAL HYGIENE

Standards of sanitation in the 18th century would be largely unacceptable today. People washed their hands and face routinely, but they rarely took full baths, and showers did not yet exist. People generally feared immersing themselves in water because they thought it would expose them to chills and infections. Louisbourg court records tell of a 50-year-old woman who fell in a pond and claimed that it was the first time in her life that she had been immersed in water.

As a result of this reluctance to take baths, many people had a strong body odour. The well-to-do, men as well as women, wore perfume to disguise the smell.

DISTRUST OF DRINKING WATER

Water is taken for granted today: turn on the tap and out it comes, hot or cold. In 18th-century Louisbourg, however, it was not so easy. Water—for cooking, washing, or drinking—came from wells. Some people were fortunate and had wells on their own property; many others had to go to public wells. Whatever well was used, the water was sometimes unsafe to drink because it was polluted, often from the well being located too close to the latrines or outhouses. As Louisbourg's water supply was not tested for bacteria or treated to ensure that it was safe for human consumption, people sometimes became ill.

Although residents realized that contaminated water contributed to the spread of disease, they did not understand why or how, as bacteria had not yet been discovered. Nonetheless, they knew enough to be cautious and often drank spruce beer instead of water. Spruce beer was made of boiled water, spruce buds, and molasses, and it had a very low alcohol content.

DOCTORS IN THE 18TH CENTURY

A doctor is someone who tries to cure the ill or injured. In the 18th century, doctors were known as surgeons or physicians. A "surgeon" treated external problems such as ulcers, wounds, or fractures and a "physician" treated internal illnesses. Physicians were much more highly regarded than surgeons, and they were also better paid. Their preferred methods of treatment included "bleeding" their patients and having them take "infusions" (liquid medicine). Surgeons, on the other hand, performed operations or applied external remedies.

During the 45-year history of Île Royale, several dozen surgeons worked in Louisbourg and other French settlements on the island, but not one physician.

SURGEONS & SURGERY

18th-century surgeon

Both military and civilian surgeons worked in
Louisbourg. The civilian surgeons looked after the
townspeople, mending broken limbs and treating
many illnesses and diseases.

Military surgeons tended to the soldiers. The military
surgeons' many duties included providing first aid,
shaving the men, checking soldiers in and out of the
hospital, visiting them weekly, and giving certificates
of disability to those who could no longer serve in the
colony. As the military surgeons looked after the
troops of the King, the King paid the surgeons'
salaries and provided the necessary instruments and
medicine.

KING'S HOSPITAL

The second largest building in Louisbourg was the
Hôpital du Roi (King's Hospital), a two-storey
masonry structure. Its perimeter was nearly 200
metres, and it had a spire of about 12 metres. The
hospital contained four wards with a total capacity of
approximately 100 beds. There were also some private
rooms, a kitchen, laundry, chapel, apothecary,
morgue, and latrines. Outside the main building was
a terrace and gardens, stable, woodshed, and bakery.
In its entirety, the King's Hospital complex occupied a
full town block.

Although the hospital was built and paid for by the
King (the government), it was operated by a religious
order, the Brothers of Charity of Saint John of God,
more commonly known as the Brothers of Charity.

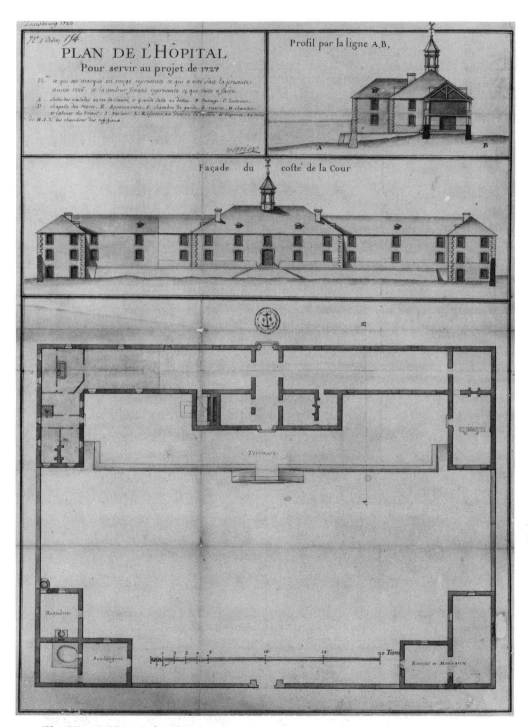

The King's Hospital

For the most part, Louisbourg's hospital was adequately furnished. From time to time, there were shortages of clean sheets and bed curtains, and problems with ventilation and light, but these difficulties were eventually overcome. The government officials who administered the building always kept a close eye on the cost of the operation.

Unlike today, women did not go to the hospital to have their babies. Instead, they had them at home, assisted by a midwife or one of the surgeons. During the 1750s, Louisbourg had an official midwife who received an annual salary from the King.

PHYSICAL FITNESS—GAMES

An easy and fun way to stay healthy is through participating in sports and games. Children in the 18th century did not have the elaborate facilities (rinks, playing fields, equipment) that boys and girls have today. Nonetheless, they certainly enjoyed playing the games of their era. Although hockey,

Nine-pin was a popular game.

soccer, basketball, or baseball did not exist per se,
some popular 18th-century games and pastimes have
persisted through the centuries essentially
unchanged.

GUESS THE GAME!

Accept this poetic challenge! Read the verses below
and guess what game or pastime is being described.

1. The children at the upper end
    Believe they will never descend,
    But down they plummet by and by.
    Fortune is changeable, and so
    All worldly favors come and go:
    When one man's low, another's high.

2. The child that's hopping in this game
    (In imitation of the lame)
    Follows the lines traced on the ground.
    He may be laboring in vain,
    For if he goes beyond the bound
    His stake becomes his rival's gain.

3. In this spectacular alignment
    They leap with luster and refinement,
    Some stooping low, some vaulting clear.
    And should you be inclined to know
    Which one puts on the finest show,
    There's no lack of eyeglasses here.

THEN & NOW—A DISCUSSION POINT

The water problems (contamination, etc.) encountered by the French at 18th-century Louisbourg are little different from those faced by many Third World countries today. Many countries are not so fortunate as Canada in having an ample supply of drinking water. Yet environmentalists maintain that Canadians even have problems (pollution and acid rain) that must be dealt with. What do you think about the world's water situation?

ANSWERS TO "GUESS THE GAME!"

1. Seesaw, or teeter-totter
2. Hopscotch
3. Leap-frog

AFTERWORD:
TODAY'S SITE

Louisbourg, the rich and colourful 18th-century
fortress, seaport, and community, is no more. It ceased
to exist long ago, except in documents and in
archaeological traces.

Yet it lives again, at least after a fashion. It stands as
the Fortress of Louisbourg National Historic Site,
located a half-hour's drive from Sydney, Cape Breton
Island, Nova Scotia.

The re-creation of Louisbourg is perhaps Canada's
most ambitious attempt to recall its 18th-century past.
Nearly one-quarter of the historic town has been
reconstructed on the site of the original settlement to
provide a sense of what is known as "living history."
Intensive research and work during the 1960s and
1970s by historians, archaeologists, architects, and
tradespeople made it possible to rebuild 50 "period"
buildings. Forges and guardhouses, homes and inns,
barracks, a bakery, and many more buildings
annually welcome tens of thousands of visitors.
People in costumes play merchants and musicians,
soldiers and servants, upper-class ladies and
gentlemen. Each one breathes life into the past.

The Fortress of Louisbourg is often rated as the top attraction in Atlantic Canada. It is a major draw for tourists from around the world, but especially for Canadians and Americans. In Cape Breton, the fortress is a major employer, as well as a source of inspiration for people interested in preserving their heritage.

SUGGESTED BOOKS, ARTICLES & VIDEOS

BOOKS & ARTICLES

There are literally hundreds of books and articles available on Louisbourg. The ones you choose to read really depends on your interests.

Would you like to read more on the cod fishery? Religious life? Gardening? The garrison? The following is a selection of some of the publications dealing with 18th-century Louisbourg.

Balcom, B.A. *The Cod Fishery of Isle Royale, 1713-1758.* Ottawa: Parks Canada, 1984.

Donovan, Kenneth, ed. *Cape Breton at 200: Essays in Honour of the Island's Bicentennial.* Sydney: UCCB Press, 1985.

————."Ile Royale, 18th-Century," Plate 24, Cole Harris, ed. *Historical Atlas of Canada.* Vol. 1. Toronto: University of Toronto Press, 1987.

————, ed. *The Island: New Perspectives in Cape Breton's History, 1713-1990.* Fredericton; Sydney: Acadiensis Press; UCCB Press, 1990.

————. "The Marquis de Chabert and the Louisbourg Observatory in the 1750s," *The American Neptune.* Vol. XLIV, No. 3: 186-97.

Dunton, Hope. *From the Hearth: Recipes from the World of 18th-Century Louisbourg.* Sydney: UCCB Press, 1986.

Fry, Bruce W. *An 'Appearance of Strength': The Fortifications of Louisbourg*. 2 vols. Ottawa: Parks Canada, 1984.

Johnston, A.J.B. *Religion in Life at Louisbourg, 1713-1758*. Montreal, Kingston: McGill-Queen's University Press, 1984.

———. *The Summer of 1744*. Ottawa: Canadian Parks Service, 1991.

McLennan, J.S. *Louisbourg from Its Foundation to Its Fall, 1713-1758*. Halifax: The Book Room, 1990.

Moore, Christopher. "How They Crossed the Ocean Accurately in 1753," *Canadian Geographic*. Vol. 101, No. 6, Dec. 1981-Jan. 1982.

———. *Louisbourg Portraits: Life in an Eighteenth-Century Garrison Town*. Toronto: Macmillan, 1982.

Nova Scotia Historical Review. Vol.10, No. 2 (1990). Five essays on Île Royale, including one on smallpox.

Proulx, Gilles. *Between France and New France: Life Aboard the Tall Sailing Ships*. Toronto; Charlottetown: Dundern Press, 1984.

Reardon, Chris, and A.J.B. Johnston. *Louisbourg: The Phoenix Fortress*. Halifax: Nimbus Publishing, 1990.

VIDEOS

There are numerous video productions dealing with Louisbourg and its history. The list below is organized by category for easy reference.

GENERAL

Louisbourg Then and Now. Canadian Broadcasting Corporation, 1982. Approx. 60 minutes. Featuring Knowlton Nash, provides a cross-section of the 18th-century town. Available in English and French from the Canadian Broadcasting Corporation, P.O. Box 500, Station A, Toronto, Ontario, M5W 1E6.

Rebuilding History. TV Ontario. Approx. 14 minutes. Looks at the historic and re-created fortress. Available from TV Ontario, P.O. Box 200, Station Q, Toronto, Ontario, M4T 2T1.

ARTISANS & TRADES

At Work in the 18th-Century. Nova Scotia Department of Education, 1989. Approx. 8 minutes. A glimpse at a wood hewer, stone cutter, carpenter, and blacksmith. Available in English and French from Education Media Services, 6955 Bayers Road, Halifax, Nova Scotia, B3L 4S5.

ASTRONOMY

Canada's Stargazers: From Louisbourg to Supernova.
Science North. Approx. 28 minutes. Focuses on
Canadian astronomical achievements, with a few
minutes on the Louisbourg observatory. Available
from Science North, 100 Ramsey Lake Road, Sudbury,
Ontario, P3E 5S9.

CHILDREN

Life in a French Fortress. TV Ontario. Approx. 14
minutes. Follows a young girl through part of a
typical 18th-century day. Animated character Trapper
hosts. Available from TV Ontario, P.O. Box 200,
Station Q, Toronto, Ontario, M4T 2T1.

CHRISTMAS

An 18th-Century Christmas. Global Communications.
Approx. 25 minutes. A glimpse at wintertime life and
moods in the fortified town. Beautiful
cinematography. Available from Global
Communications, 81 Greene Road, Don Mills,
Ontario, M3C 2A2.

CLOTHING & FASHION

Getting Dressed in the 18th Century. Nova Scotia
Department of Education. 1989. Approx. 12 minutes.
Available in English and French from Education
Media Services, 6955 Bayers Road, Halifax, Nova
Scotia, B3L 4S5.

COOKING

Cooking in an 18th-Century Kitchen. Nova Scotia Department of Education, 1989. Approx. 15 minutes. An evening meal is prepared by a busy kitchen staff. Available in English and French from Education Media Services, 6955 Bayers Road, Halifax, Nova Scotia, B3L 4S4.

MILITARY LIFE

Les compagnies franches de la Marine. National Film Board. Approx. 13 minutes. Examines the life of a typical soldier. Available in English and French from the nearest office of the National Film Board of Canada. Production no. 106C 0180 532.

RECONSTRUCTION

Louisbourg. National Film Board, 1972. Approx. 30 minutes. Treats both 18th-century history and 20th-century reconstruction. Available in English and French from the nearest office of the National Film Board of Canada. Production no. 106C 0172 553.

ACKNOWLEDGEMENTS

Albert Bridge teacher Cathy Lawrence first suggested that Louisbourg's history deserved to be better taught and understood in the classrooms of Atlantic Canada. Mrs. Lawrence discussed her concerns with Bill O'Shea, head of historical resources at the Fortress of Louisbourg National Historic Site, and with Nancy Nicol, supervisor of curriculum with the Cape Breton District School Board. In the days that followed, a number of teachers under the jurisdiction of the school board were selected to serve on a committee to develop material that could be used in classrooms across the country.

A large thank-you goes to the Nova Scotia Teachers Union, which awarded two grants from the Program Development Assistance Fund to help pay for design, typesetting, and other costs. Similarly, Enterprise Cape Breton Corporation helped make the book a reality by agreeing to purchase copies of the text, which it then generously donated to various schools.

A debt of gratitude also goes to Bernie Hart of the Nova Scotia Department of Education. Because of his support, fortress staff were able to work with Ray Whitley and others in Education Media Services to produce a series of videos that supplement this book. (A list of those videos is provided in the previous section.)

ILLUSTRATION CREDITS

Many of the illustrations in this book came from the Fortress of Louisbourg National Historic Site. Others came from the following archives, libraries, museums and books, which we gratefully acknowledge:

Archives Nationales (France): 6, 9, 68, 114, 133
Bellin. *Le petit atlas maritime* (1764): 35
Bibliothèque de l'Arsenal (Paris): 20
Bibliothèque Nationale (Paris): 36, 39, 44, 57, 113
Congrégation de Notre-Dame (Montreal): 99
Diderot and D'Alembert, eds. *L'encyclopédie, ou dictionnaire raisonné des sciences, des arts et des métiers* (1751-65): 11, 70, 71, 77, 103, 110, 120, 121, 131, 132
Duhamel Du Monceau. *Traité général des pesches ...* (1769-77): 56, 60, 61, 62, 83
Library of Congress (Washington): 43
Ministère de la Défense, Service Historique de l'Armée de Terre (France): 14, 15, 21, 76, 79, 80
Musée de la Marine (Paris): 122
Newberry Library (Chicago): 78
Period engravings: 67, 69, 129, 135
Reardon. *Louisbourg: The Phoenix Fortress:* vi, 87 (bottom), 102, 107, 134
University College of Cape Breton (Sydney), courtesy Lewis Parker 49, 50